The Beatles Invasion

THE INSIDE STORY OF THE TWO-WEEK TOUR
THAT ROCKED AMERICA

BY BOB SPITZ

Contents

ABOUT THE AUTHOR

A longtime rock 'n' roll insider, Bob Spitz is a veteran journalist, screenwriter and best-selling biographer whose books include *The Beatles* (2005) and *Dearie: The Remarkable Life of Julia Child* (2012). He is currently at work on a life of Ronald Reagan.

The Revolution Begins

BEATLEMANIA: America never saw it coming.
As 1963 tided into '64, the '60s had yet to find a definable beat. There was no counterculture, no Age of Aquarius, no Maui Wowie, no yeah-yeah-yeah. "Far out" defined a distant point on the horizon, "groovy" a woodworker's dilemma. But the times, as the poet said, were a-changin'.

On Feb. 7, 1964, as the Beatles boarded Pan Am Flight 101 in London for their first U.S. visit, they had little idea what lay in store for them.

A cultural shift had begun to jolt the country's tectonic plates, from its glossy surface down to its disenchanted core. Young people were struggling to find a means of self-expression. Traditional values were on their way out, but nobody knew yet what was coming in. Even so, a momentum was clearly building. The buttoned-down Eisenhower era, a cushion against postwar uncertainty, was giving way to a ferment of social restlessness and a generation waiting to break loose—and to experiment.

Upstarts were already rattling the gates of the establishment. In 1963, Betty Friedan ignited discontented housewives with *The Feminine Mystique*, claiming that modern women craved meaningful lives, careers, sex, R-E-S-P-E-C-T. The civil-rights movement, inspired by Martin Luther King Jr., challenged the conscience of the country, and college students poured into the South, committed to actively dismantling segregation. The threat of thermonuclear war and talk of a widening "missile gap" aroused interest in pacifism, while the escalation of America's military involvement in Southeast Asia heightened opposition to the draft and touched off a crusade against violence and authority.

Although the process was liberating, it was wrenching, too. The country was still in mourning for a youthful president who was the face of its new ideals. It was little more than two months after John F. Kennedy's assassination when the Beatles first landed in New York. According to Dan Daniel, a longtime local DJ who stood among the waiting crowd, "America needed something uplifting, and we were ready to smile."

Illustration by Sean McCabe

They were about to get exactly that, and in spades.

It seems impossible to recall a time when the Beatles weren't part of our collective consciousness. Yet Feb. 7 marks the day—exactly 50 years ago—when they went from being beside the point to beloved. In an era when 15 minutes of fame seems just about right and pop music is as disposable as Pop-Tarts, the Beatles endure. "Their songs have shaped all of our lives," says Graham Nash, who, as a member of the Hollies, played on double bills with the Beatles at the legendary Cavern, in Liverpool. "They're like the crown jewels; their value is incalculable." Beatles songs are a daily part of our lives, played in every conceivable setting, in nurseries and school assemblies, over department-store loudspeakers, at celebrations, in elevators and ads, on the radio. Their music, as well as their image, is an indelible trust. Their 187 songs make up a canon, much like Beethoven's nine symphonies or Shakespeare's 38 plays. Universities analyze their careers, historians their lasting appeal.

Yet until just a few weeks before the Beatles touched down in New York, no British rock 'n' roll act had cracked America's insular charts. "We didn't think we stood a chance," John Lennon recalled. To the Beatles, a trip to America gave credence to the flat-earth theory; as explorers to the New World, they might fall off the edge. In fact, Cliff Richard, the U.K.'s reigning megastar, had bombed on an American tour. "He was 14th on the bill with Frankie Avalon," John complained, with some exaggeration. Even so, how were the Beatles to expect better than Cliff?

At best, they fretted, it was a high-stakes gamble. Over the previous nine months they had scored three No. 1 singles on the U.K. charts; they were the darlings of London. There was something quintessentially British about these uncompromising musicians, these charismatic, cheeky, shaggy-haired boys from the north of England. A word had been coined to mark their popularity: *Beatlemania*. Their appearances had reached that manic state. As John might have quipped, "Why risk all that on abroad?" Then again, they'd recently blown Tommy Roe and Chris Montez, two visiting Yanks, off the stage during a tour. "The Beatles could take it to the Americans," proclaimed the British rock rag *Melody Maker*, but no one was willing to put money on that horse.

O F COURSE, EVERYONE won big when they crossed the finish line. The Beatles took the colonies by storm, and American teenagers' lives changed instantly—and forever. "It was the most amazing thing I'd ever experienced," the ageless Ronnie Spector of the Ronettes told TIME recently. "One day, nobody in the States had any idea who they were; the next day, every kid was a Beatle fanatic."

Those kids, of course, are now card-carrying boomers, with children and even grandchildren who share the same passion. The Beatles remain relevant, timeless, seemingly invulnerable to trends. *Will you still love me when I'm 64?* The 14-year-olds who first laid eyes on the mop-tops on *The Ed Sullivan Show* can now answer affirmatively with shocking precision. "What's most interesting to me is that our records are still coming out, and they're the same records, and the new generation gets to hear them," said Ringo Starr on the occasion of his 70th—yes, *70th*—birthday, in 2010. "That's the most important thing to me. The music we make, it's still going on."

Fifty years later, their stock is a solid blue-chip commodity. In 2009, Nielsen SoundScan named the Beatles' *1* the best-selling album of the decade—and that was two years before it was released digitally. Concerts of the surviving members, Paul McCartney and Ringo, are still drawing sold-out crowds. The Beatles version of the Rock Band video game was an international sensation, although Paul complained, "My grandkids always beat me. And I say, 'Listen, you may beat me at Rock Band, but I made the original records, so shut up.'"

Honors continue to roll in—stars on the Hollywood Walk of Fame, induction into the Rock and Roll Hall of Fame, a knighthood for Paul, a minor planet named after Ringo, a corner of New York's Central Park dedicated to John's memory, a George Harrison biopic directed by no less than Martin Scorsese. Tribute bands abound. Paul picked up a 2012 Grammy for his LP *Kisses on the Bottom.* Along with Elvis, the Beatles top the list of most-forged autographs.

Even the Vatican has finally forgiven them for their helter-skelter lifestyles and John's 1966 claim that they were "more popular than Jesus." According to *L'Osservatore Romano,* the Holy See's newspaper, "It's true they lived dissolute and uninhibited lives. But listening to their songs, all of this seems distant and meaningless. Their beautiful melodies, which changed forever pop music and still give us emotions, live on like precious jewels."

BUT IN LATE 1963, to a group of hard-charging Liverpool lads, the jewel in the crown—a hit American record—seemed elusive, unattainable. Two tiny U.S. independent labels had released a string of Beatles singles that, despite glowing reviews, went nowhere fast. Radio airplay was as scarce as plutonium; disc jockeys ignored them completely. And Capitol, the American subsidiary of the Beatles' English label, EMI, repeatedly refused to put out any of their records. All efforts to change Capitol's mind might as well have fallen on deaf ears. Its official reply: "Not suitable for the U.S. market."

Not suitable for the U.S. market. That verdict haunted the lads. Even when "She Loves You" amassed advance orders in the U.K. for a record-setting 500,000 copies—a figure so enormous that even EMI was impressed—the Beatles resisted the temptation to schedule an American tour. They'd put their collective feet down when Brian Epstein, their devoted manager, proposed such a trip. "Not until we mean something there," they insisted, "not until we have a No. 1."

John was discouraged. "The thing is, in America, it just seemed ridiculous," he recalled, "I mean, the idea of having a hit record over there. It was just something you could never do."

A swirl of forces was starting to converge, however. Ringo claimed that "the gods were on our side," but an unlikelier lot of deities is hard to imagine. TV host Ed Sullivan, disc jockey Carroll James and impresario Sid Bernstein had nothing in common aside from showbiz credentials and musical taste rooted in the big-band era. Yet by November 1963, to start the machinery in motion, each of these American men had stepped outside his natural habitat to endorse a rock 'n' roll band from Liverpool. The Beatles did their part, too, by releasing a new single, "I Want to Hold Your Hand"—a song so utterly joyous and undeniable that even the recalcitrant Capitol Records was defenseless against its charm.

But America still seemed a distant port of call. In January 1964 the Beatles were stationed in Paris, playing a three-week residency at the Olympia Theater, where indifferent French audiences made them reevaluate their universal appeal. They'd also discovered Bob Dylan, whose music was a revelation, if not flat-out unsettling; vocally and poetically, it turned the Beatles inside out. A lot of *je ne sais quoi* collided backstage in France. How might their music gracefully evolve? Were they ready to push across new frontiers?

"One night," Paul recalled, "we arrived back at the hotel from the Olympia, when a telegram came through to Brian from Capitol Records … He came running into the room saying, 'Hey, look! You are No. 1 in America.'"

Ready or not, it was time for the Beatles to pack their bags.

Yeah, Yeah,

HERE WE GO

As the Beatles hit American soil for the first time, photographer Harry Benson snapped them leaving the plane at JFK airport. The first stirrings of Beatlemania had reached the U.S. even before they had.

Yeah!

"In Liverpool, when you stood on the edge of the water you knew the next place was America,"

John Lennon mused much later while reflecting on his first visit, in 1964. He was enchanted as a child by the prospect of the States, its mystery and romance, its promise of opportunity. Everything he dreamed about lay somewhere out there, over the horizon: Brando, the Beats, rock 'n' roll—especially rock 'n' roll. It was the land of his forefathers: Chuck, Elvis, Richard, Buddy, Phil and Don. Now, however, as Pan Am Flight 101 approached New York, he fidgeted in his seat, unable to deal with the reality of touching down there, at long last.

The Beatles' fate in America was still up for grabs. They were entering a musical and cultural scene that was in unprecedented flux, with sharper generational divides than ever before. There were two musical forces, and it was still unclear which would triumph: acts that were the mainstay of nightclubs and establishment venues like *The Ed Sullivan Show*, or young upstarts who were trying to hijack the scene. The old guard and holdovers from Tin Pan Alley—Andy Williams, Connie Francis, Perry Como, even Bobby Vinton and Brenda Lee—were still per-

OFF TO THE BIG TIME

John and his wife Cynthia on the flight to New York. John knew that success in the U.S. would legitimize the Beatles in a way that no British band had experienced.

forming sedate standards and continued to dominate airplay. In the weeks before the Beatles arrived, the Singing Nun and Vinton topped the American charts. Young stars with a musical edge, though, were starting to make some inroads. New sounds were emerging—the Beach Boys and Stevie Wonder were finding their voices—but rock 'n' roll in America was still waiting for someone to deliver the juice.

Amid all this ferment, the Beatles had been heard in the U.S. but never seen, a factor that troubled John as well as his bandmates. Would kids there buy into their act? Would Beatle-mania survive the trip overseas? It was hard to compute after their sendoff from London. Four thousand kids had swarmed Heathrow that morning, Feb. 7, 1964, as the boys boarded the plane to the newly named JFK International Airport. They'd staged a prearranged tableau for the loyal fans, pausing on their way across the tarmac, then turning on cue and waving in unison. It triggered a typical Pavlovian response, Beatles style: the crowd went nuts, screaming and cheering, the Beatles laughing and shouting right back at them. How could the boys expect to duplicate such love and excitement in the States? Anything less would be a major letdown.

John calculated the Beatles' odds as the plane began its descent. He stared dolefully at the seat back in front of him, clutching the hand of his wife Cynthia. There were so many variables that would determine their success: whether "I Want to Hold Your Hand," released in late December, would sustain its initial impact in the States; how tickets there were selling for their upcoming concerts; whether their appearances on *The Ed Sullivan Show* would capture the imagination of American teenagers. Would anyone even care?

Backstage with Roy Orbison (right) and Gerry and the Pacemakers during a U.K. tour in May 1963. The Beatles soon replaced Orbison at the top of the bill.

John knew the score: America had the aura. It would legitimize the Beatles in a way that no one from England had yet experienced. British bands hardly did more than cover the latest American hits, their versions too mainstream, too lightweight, lacking the fire of rock 'n' roll. It never occurred to them to let it rip or to write their own songs. Even the Beatles' early sets owed everything to the Coasters, the Shirelles, Chuck Berry, the Marvelettes, Arthur Alexander. When it came to rock 'n' roll, there was no competition: America had invented it and seemed to have cornered the market. But the balance of power was beginning to shift.

THE BEAT SCENE, as it was called, was thriving in Liverpool, where a colony of coffee bars and dance halls served as incubators for rock 'n' roll. Slightly more than 300 Liverpool bands caught up in the nascent club life sought their precious piece of the rock. There was no mistaking that a distinctive sound was developing, a unique, idiosyncratic pop style that would come to be known as Mersey Beat, after the dark, choppy river that is the city's lifeblood. The music had a rough-edged working-class sensibility, with catchy melodies, clever lyrics, seamless three-part harmonies, nimble instrumentation and dynamic chords dropped into a pattern that remade a tired form. It was the blast that set off the British rock revolution, and the Beatles were the spark that lit its fuse.

Ingeniously, the Beatles had assembled elements from their favorite American hits, borrow-

From American music...

Clockwise from top left: Gene Vincent, the Everly Brothers, Buddy Holly, Little Richard, Chuck Berry, Eddie Cochran

...to the British sound

Clockwise from top left: The Rolling Stones, the Hollies, Dusty Springfield, the Kinks, Eric Clapton and the Yardbirds, the Animals, Billy J. Kramer and the Dakotas

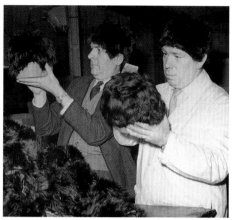

TOPPERMOST OF THE POPPERMOST

By 1963, Beatles fever was raging in Britain. Clockwise from top left: Victorious ticket holders; Beatles wigs, which reportedly outsold these merchants' 2,000-a-day supply; a portrait of the band by Norman Parkinson; tending to a fan who fainted (next to her is a note with a song request), while John performs. Opposite: Bill for a concert of Mersey Beat bands managed by Brian Epstein.

ing from the Everly Brothers, Eddie Cochran, Buddy Holly and Gene Vincent, giving the alloy a bold new touch. Fellow Scousers Gerry and the Pacemakers, the Searchers, and Billy J. Kramer and the Dakotas helped to refine the sound and contributed to the groundswell. But the music couldn't be contained in Liverpool; it was contagious, seeping into surrounding cities—places like Manchester, Leeds, Sheffield and Birmingham—where hometown pop heroes picked up the beat. Then, in 1963, the whole scene cracked wide open. The Yardbirds (featuring guitarist Eric Clapton), the Pretty Things, the Animals, the Kinks, Freddie and the Dreamers, Dusty

Springfield and two bands from London, the Dave Clark Five and the Rolling Stones, began churning out original hits, none of which imitated American rock 'n' roll so much as adapted it in ways that brought new energy to the form. By 1964, as historian Greg Shaw noted, "it seemed that England had exploded with a completely new and revolutionary approach to rock 'n' roll."

But no one epitomized it like the Beatles. They had everything—the look, the sound, the personality, great songs, tremendous showmanship and the ability to put it all together. In person, they played their hearts out; their shows jacked up audiences to the point of hysteria. Every record they made seemed genuinely fresh and unspoiled by commercialism. Kids across the country were gripped by the excitement, gobbling up records and concert tickets at an unprecedented pace. "To those of us in England who lived for the next great American single," recalled journalist Ray Connolly, "it seemed like the Beatles were the promise we'd been waiting for all our lives."

Beatlemania was sweeping England when Brian Epstein decided to test its legs. In November 1963, he spent a week visiting New York City to gauge the extent of the Beatles' popularity. At the time, they had fairly hijacked the U.K. charts: "She Loves You" was embedded at No. 1; their second studio album, *With the Beatles*, was poised to be another chart topper, with 500,000 preorders before its Nov. 22 release; and Billy J. Kramer's version of "I'll Keep You Satisfied," written by John and Paul, was inching up at No. 4. United Artists had signed them to a splashy movie deal. And merchandising offers were pouring in. But in New York, Epstein came up against cold reality. On the city's mean streets it was as if the band didn't exist. He canvassed the record stores along Broadway without unearthing a single Beatles disc. There wasn't a mention of them, it seemed, anywhere on the continent. And when he called Capitol Records to confirm an appointment to discuss the Beatles, a receptionist asked: "Are they affiliated with a label?"

To soften the blows, Epstein had wangled a meeting with the impresario Ed Sullivan, whose television variety show was a Sunday-night ritual as well as a surefire star-making vehicle. Sullivan, a former entertainment columnist, recognized a hot scoop when he saw one, and over dinner at the Hotel Delmonico he proposed what was then an extravagant deal for the Beatles: three appearances on his show at a fee of $4,500 per performance, plus five round-trip airline tickets and all their expenses while they were in America.

The offer, Epstein knew, was as good as gold, but it wouldn't be worth a sou without a record in release. And at that moment, the Beatles' prospects seemed hopeless. All attempts to launch their records in the States were scotched. Capitol, EMI's American affiliate, continued to regard them as foreign undesirables. Every two weeks EMI sent their records, along with reams of publicity extolling the boys' godlike status, and within days got back the same terse rejection: *Not suitable for the American market.*

Frustrated by Capitol's rigid resistance, EMI entrusted a feisty New York lawyer named Paul Marshall to license the Beatles elsewhere in the hope that a more discerning American company would hear the goods. Incredibly, all the major labels—RCA, Columbia, Atlantic, London, Mercury, United Artists—passed. So Marshall turned to the smaller independents, landing a deal with Vee-Jay, a Chicago R&B label with an impressive pedigree. Vee-Jay had recently peeled off a blistering streak of hits: "Duke of Earl" by Gene Chandler, a million-seller by Jerry Butler called "He Will Break Your Heart," "Raindrops" by Dee Clark, with crossover sensations the Four Seasons contributing "Sherry," "Big Girls Don't Cry" and "Walk Like a Man." But days before a release could be mounted, Vee-Jay's president went on a weekend bender in Las Vegas and for all intents and purposes gambled away the company.

Even so, Vee-Jay managed to release two singles, "Please Please Me" and "From Me to You," that went nowhere fast. American disc jockeys weren't impressed; airplay was scarce—and scarcer. Before a third record was due out, Marshall gave Capitol yet another chance to salvage its inherited stake. But the label's primary tastemaker, an A&R man named Dave Dexter, delivered what amounted to the coup de grâce. The Beatles, he said, were "stone-cold dead in the U.S. marketplace."

Desperate to make something happen, Marshall cut a sweetheart deal—of sorts—with a small Philadelphia label, Swan Records, to issue the next Beatles release. Swan "didn't pay anything to license it," an EMI executive recalled. "They just guaranteed to put the bloody thing out, as a favor to us."

The bloody thing, however, happened to be a gem. While on tour in Newcastle, Paul had sketched out a lyric fragment, a call-and-response, with a nonsensical but effective hook. As it stood, he would sing, "She loves you," whereby the rest of the band would respond, "Yeah … yeah … yeah," a gimmick they initially dismissed as a "crummy idea." But one day's "crummy" is the next day's "swell," and after a rewrite back at the Turks Head Hotel, the song shaped up as a prospective smash. George Martin, the group's producer, previewed a rough draft at Abbey Road studios and declared it "brilliant … one of the most vital [songs] the Beatles had written so far."

In fact, "She Loves You," as recorded, was a flat-out classic, the performance a knockout that captivates even today. What the Beatles built into the song provided a lasting image: the "yeah … yeah … yeah"s and the falsetto "ooooo"s became instant iconic symbols. No matter how their music evolved, no matter how they experimented with complex textures and electronics, it's hard to think of the Beatles without visualizing them as four grinning moptops in that classic stage pose—the guitars riding high on their chests, drumsticks rhythmically pummeling the cymbals—singing, "And you know you should be glad—*ooooooooo*," followed by a decisive shake of their beautiful hair. Nothing identifies them more vividly.

Trouble was, you can't see into a record. And unable to give listeners the chance to experience the Beatles' charisma, the Swan version of "She Loves You" took an early swan dive. Even Dick Clark, the pop tastemaker of *American Bandstand*, told desperate Swan reps

The arriving travelers go through customs at Kennedy airport. Opposite: "She Loves You" was a million-seller in Britain, but Swan Records' American release had a hard time getting anywhere.

that "it'll never fly." Nevertheless, he previewed it on *Bandstand*'s "Rate-a-Record" segment, where it earned a wretched 71 out of a possible 98 points. "I figured these guys were going nowhere," he recalled.

Except that in England they were going through the roof—to the toppermost of the poppermost, as the Beatles dubbed it. As sales of "She Loves You" shot over the magic million mark and a million advance orders poured in for their next single, EMI ran out of patience with its American sharecroppers. No more "Would you put out the Beatles' new record?" EMI insisted that Capitol "*must* take it." Case closed.

Must: the ultimatum steamed Capitol's buns. Never, in their long relationship, had the brother labels breached each other's autonomy. But, fortunately, the offending record was a gift from the rock gods. "I Want to Hold Your Hand" was unlike anything Capitol had ever heard, a two-and-a-half-minute rave-up that practically jumped off the grooves. Hard-nosed and unsparing, the song revealed everything that was remarkable about the Beatles: a pure pop lyric, slashing vocals, an overheated arrangement and enough energy to power the average supertanker. If Capitol was forced to launch the Beatles in America, then at least this was a record the company could get behind.

But grudgingly. A January release was announced with a measly pressing of 5,000 copies. No use overextending for a certain stiff. And that might have been the end of it, were it not for a grenade lobbed into the mix. In mid-November, TV crews for CBS and NBC brought back footage from England that showcased Beatlemania in its full regalia. In two four- or five-minute film segments, Americans finally got the lay of the land, from the haircuts to the screaming kids to the "yeah ... yeah ... yeah"s. A teenager from Maryland named Marsha Albert watched the footage and dashed off a letter to her local DJ at WWDC in Washington, D.C. "I heard about the Beatles on the Evening News," she wrote. "Why can't we have music like that in America?"

"Why not?" said Carroll James, a genial straight arrow who played a mixed bag of pop standards on his nightly show. Granted, the Beatles didn't jibe with the station's Frank Sinatra–Nat King Cole fare, but maybe it was time to shake things up. Intrigued, James persuaded a BOAC flight attendant to import a U.K. copy of "I Want to Hold Your Hand," and on Dec. 17, 1963, he invited Marsha Albert to introduce it on the air, the first time it was ever played in the U.S. After the final "ha-a-a-a-a-and," "the switchboard just went totally wild," James recalled, so he "played it again in the next hour, which is something I'd never done before."

WWDC touched off a wave of Beatlemania that rippled across the country. Radio stations jumped impetuously on the bandwagon; teenagers laid siege to stores for copies of the record. The suits at Capitol didn't know what had hit them. In a desperate move to salvage a potential catastrophe, the label moved up the release to Dec. 26. Three days later, it had sold 250,000 copies.

The Beatles had a beachhead in America.

Now, as their plane banked sharply over the eastern shore of Long Island, John glanced across the aisle at Paul, George and Ringo huddling at a window. They were giddy with anticipation. It had been a lively eight-hour flight across the Atlantic. The plane had been packed with an entourage of Beatles disciples—friends, reporters, photographers, henchmen, hangers-on, hucksters who hoped to make a buck off their hides. Even the ever-paranoid Phil Spector, who famously refused to fly, had hitched a ride home from London, on the hunch that a plane carrying cargo as precious as the Beatles wouldn't dare crash. But all John could focus on at the moment was the next two weeks in America—and not crashing while there.

Much worry had been expended over their reception in the States, beginning with their arrival. Documentary filmmaker Albert Maysles, who with his brother, David, had been hired only that morning to shoot a chronicle of the Beatles' visit, recalled, "No one could be sure whether there would be five people or 5,000 people showing up at the airport." But minutes before landing, news filtered from the cockpit through the plane that helped to put their minds at ease. As Paul remembered it: "The pilot had rung ahead and said, 'Tell the boys there's a big crowd waiting for them.'"

From the air, the terminals looked jittery, alive. A swarm of locusts? No. Wall-to-wall kids, who had scrambled over barricades and fences to get a look at the Beatles. Applause and cheers broke out inside the plane. Even John, whose face had been a brittle mask since takeoff, allowed himself a reassured grin. "Just look at that!" one of the Beatles murmured.

> **A REPORTER, COWED BY THE SCENE, STAMMERED: "NO ONE, I MEAN NO ONE, HAS EVER SEEN OR EVEN REMOTELY SUSPECTED ANYTHING LIKE THIS BEFORE!"**

All morning long, New York DJs, broadcasting live from the airport, had exhorted listeners to join the throng, promising interviews and prizes: T-shirts, Beatles wigs, photographs, records—and, best of all, a close-up glimpse of the British sensations. The appeals touched off a virtual five-borough stampede, so that by noon the Pan Am terminal was a migrant teenage encampment. The airline's observation deck bulged to capacity. The *New York Times* reported that "three thousand teenagers stood four deep on the upper arcade of the International Arrivals Building ... girls, girls and more girls." Police, overwhelmed by the crowd, fought to hold the kids in check as fans flung themselves against (and sometimes over) the barricades.

Just before 1:30 p.m., Flight 101 taxied to a stop outside the terminal and the aircraft door popped open. An explosion of cheers and screams rang out as the crowd stormed forward.

There, at last, they were—the Beatles! First George (soon to be 21), then John (23), followed by Paul (21) and Ringo (23)—and, yes, they were a sight to behold. Four winsome, outrageously long-haired young men in identical dark overcoats, grinning ear to ear and waving to the crowd. The spectacle of them touched off a fresh wave of pandemonium.

"The four Beatles have left the airplane," Paul Parker, a WINS reporter, shouted into his microphone. "There's that *fabulous* hairdo. And one of them is standing and he's jumping and he's wiggling and he's waving his fingers! *Oh, look at him wiggle!* It's almost impossible to describe!"

Another reporter, cowed by the scene, stammered: "No one, I mean no one, has ever seen or even remotely suspected anything like this before!"

He got that right. Not for kings or visiting dignitaries or even celebrities. The display at JFK was an entirely new phenomenon.

"We heard that our records were selling well in America," George noted (Capitol announced that they were the fastest-selling in the label's history), "but it wasn't until we stepped off the plane ... that we understood what was going on. Seeing thousands of kids there to meet us made us realize just how popular we were there."

From left: Devotees at the airport in their finery; back home in Britain, newspapers closely followed the big stateside event.

Everywhere, perhaps, but with the pool of hard-boiled reporters who had been waiting for hours to cover these British intruders. More than 200 of them were crammed into Pan Am's smoke-filled lounge, grumbling about the lousy assignment, when the Beatles finally paraded into the room. Like a cavalry charge, the reporters opened fire, question after question without letup, until it all just fused into babble.

Brian Sommerville, the band's new press officer, tried desperately to impose order but eventually succumbed to shouting back. "All right then. Shut up!" he insisted. "Just shut up!"

"Yeah, yeah, everybody just *sharrup*," barked John, which stunned the crowd into applause.

What now? The press and the Beatles stared awkwardly at each other until a reporter managed to break the ice. "Will you sing something for us?"

"*No!*" the Beatles shouted in unison.

"We need money first," John shot back.

Wha ...? These boys were witty. The frost in the lounge started to melt.

"What do you think of Beethoven?"

"Great," Ringo answered, "especially his poems."

Oh, this was too much! The New York press fell into a veritable swoon. "We'd learnt the whole game," John recalled. "We knew how to handle the press when we arrived." But it had never been handled like this before.

"Are you for real?" a reporter wondered.

"Come and have a feel."

"Do you hope to get a haircut?"

"I had one yesterday," George said with a grin, displaying his generous mane.

It went on like that for almost an hour, a spontaneous Abbott and Costello–type routine, with the cynical press corps as willing straight men. Whatever the press expected from these boys, it was completely unprepared for what it got. The Beatles were irresistible; they made great copy.

As everyone prepared to head for the exits, Paul commandeered the mike. "We have a message," he announced with great significance. The reporters flipped their notebooks back open, as photographers pressed in to get the crucial shot. "Our message is: buy more Beatles records!"

As tomorrow's newspapers would confirm, the Beatles had taken New York by storm.

GUITAR HEROES

A fan touches a Beatles instrument case as a chauffeur is removing it from a limo. The band had to make a run for it to get from the car to the Plaza Hotel door.

Mania in Manhattan

The Beatles were gobsmacked. New York City seemed a world unto itself, and as they limoed in from JFK, its wonders unfolded.

The radio, for one thing, symbolized the city's fabulousness. At the airport, Pepsi had given each of the Beatles a transistor radio, and throughout the trip in, they flitted from station to station, unable to wrap their heads around it.

"We were so overawed by American radio," John confessed. In England there was only one station, the stodgy BBC, which basically ignored the type of music the Beatles craved. Suddenly it was all at their fingertips—a nonstop jukebox of those American R&B hits they'd been dying to hear: Marvin Gaye, Smokey Robinson, the Shirelles, the Ronettes. And sandwiched between each two, a *Beatles record*!

"I remember ... hearing a running commentary on *us*," Paul recalled. "'They have just left the airport and are coming toward New York City.' It was like a dream. The greatest fantasy ever."

As the cultural capital of America, New York offered it all—theater, television and the music scene, which ran the gamut of taste and inventiveness but also reflected the sweeping changes of the time. Uptown, the city was opening Lincoln Center, a new mecca for classical

FROM ON HIGH

Waving to the public from their hotel suite. After the Beatles checked in, the crowds ballooned till the sidewalks in front of the building were a solid block of humanity.

music. And on Broadway, audiences packed the house for shows such as *Hello, Dolly!*, which had just opened. *Funny Girl* was slated to bow in March, with a new vocalist named Barbra Streisand. But downtown was where the real fermentation was happening. The club scene had exploded, and folk singers were battling it out with jazz greats for control of the turf. The Village Gate showcased an astonishing array of innovators such as Thelonious Monk, Charles Mingus, Nina Simone and Dizzy Gillespie. Bob Dylan was a regular at Gerde's Folk City and the Gaslight, sharing stage time with Joan Baez, Phil Ochs, Tom Paxton, Dave Van Ronk, Judy Collins and Ramblin' Jack Elliott.

By the time the Beatles' car made its way from JFK to Manhattan, word was out and fans had already begun to mob the posh Plaza Hotel on Fifth Avenue.

Incredibly, it was only then discovered that several guests—Mr. J. Lennon, Mr. P. McCartney, Mr. G. Harrison and Mr. R. Starkey—having booked reservations under their own names, were in fact the same Beatles splashed across the news. By the time management found out, it was too late to do anything about it. Reluctantly, the boys were shown to a spacious 10-room suite on the 12th floor with commanding views of Central Park.

To the Beatles, it was heaven—a TV in every room, a fully stocked bar, no end of luxuries—and hell: absolutely no place to go. The fans outside had hemmed the boys in, making any excursion just plain foolhardy. "We're like prisoners," John told Ronnie Bennett (now Ronnie Spector), who had called him soon after he'd checked in.

One week earlier her group, the Ronettes, had been in England, promoting their smash hit "Be My Baby." The Beatles, diehard fans of the girls, were scarcely out of their sight. The boys found the Ronettes as exotic as they were attractive. In fact, John, a married man, had been seeing Ronnie on the sly, while George dated her sister, Estelle. The situation was all the more dicey with Ronnie's Svengali boyfriend, Phil Spector, a highly excitable fixture on the scene. "When the Beatles knew they were heading to the States for the first time, they asked the Ronettes to come as their escorts," Ronnie remembers. "To be with the Beatles as they go to the U.S.! They *begged* us." But the jealous Spector forbade it and sent them home early from London. He was equally worried about the Beatles' impact on the American music scene, she maintains: "He loved the Beatles, but he knew they were taking his spotlight away."

> TO THE BEATLES, IT WAS HEAVEN— A TV IN EVERY ROOM, A FULLY STOCKED BAR, NO END OF LUXURIES— AND HELL: ABSOLUTELY NO PLACE TO GO. THE FANS OUTSIDE HAD HEMMED THE BOYS IN, MAKING ANY EXCURSION JUST PLAIN FOOLHARDY.

In New York, John again sought the Ronettes' companionship, only this time as a hedge against the shut-in. So Friday night, the three young women fought their way into the Plaza. The crowds had ballooned since the Beatles checked in. The sidewalks in front of the building were a solid block of humanity. Chants of "*We want the Beatles! We want the Beatles!*" punctuated the New York din. "It seemed like the whole world was outside that hotel," Ronnie recalls. "It actually scared me. I felt like I'd wandered into another world."

Upstairs, however, was a picture of relative calm. "It was such a cool scene," says DJ Dan Daniel, who lingered in the corridor. "No hullabaloo. The door to their suite was left open. You could just come and go as you pleased." Press wandered in and out, various well-wishers, Brian Epstein. And in the middle of it all, the Beatles and the Ronettes, sitting on the floor, oblivious to the sur-

ARMY OF FANS

In hopes of a Beatles sighting, their admirers clogged the streets in front of the Plaza throughout the band's stay.

WITH THE BEATLES

READY FOR THEIR CLOSE-UP

Photographer: Bill Eppridge

 "He never talked about photographing the Beatles," says Adrienne Aurichio of her husband, Bill Eppridge, who died in October 2013 at the age of 75. "In the mid-'90s I was pulling photos for a *Life* magazine project, and some had Bill's name on them. After knowing him for eight years, I was still discovering all the amazing things he had done for the magazine: Vietnam, Woodstock, Needle Park, the shooting of Bobby Kennedy [Eppridge took the iconic photo of Kennedy being comforted by busboy Juan Romero]. In fact, Bill had just returned from photographing the imperial wizard of the United Klans of America when he was asked to go to the airport to shoot these young British musicians. Bill said their banter at the press conference was the funniest thing he had ever seen, so he decided to stick with the story. Inside the Plaza suite he came face to face with Ringo, who said, 'OK, Mr. *Life* magazine, what can we do for you?' Part of Bill's charm was to be unobtrusive so people felt comfortable, which you can see in the shot of the Beatles listening to a playback of a BBC telephone interview. Ninety rolls of film later, he helped us see the Beatles take America by storm. You see it in the faces of the kids; on the face of Ed Sullivan, who was clearly delighted by them. Everyone went away feeling good." Bill Eppridge's *The Beatles: Six Days That Changed the World*, coedited by Aurichio, will be available in February 2014. "He got to see the finished book before he died," she says, "and he was really happy with it."

HELP FROM THEIR FRIENDS

Above: The high-octane Murray the K and Beatles friend Estelle Bennett of the Ronettes (the group is shown left) made their way into the hotel to visit the boys, who felt like "prisoners." Opposite: By Saturday, George was in bed with a fever.

rounding stir. "They had a little record player and stacks of records, lots of R&B stuff," Ronnie says. They harmonized with their favorite American hits. A plate of the crustless cucumber tea sandwiches the Beatles loved got passed and refilled many times over. "We were all just a couple of kids enjoying ourselves."

In between, the Beatles couldn't keep their hands off the radio. "We phoned every [station] in town," John recalled. They gorged on the music, making requests in return for a recorded station promo. One source of their repeated high jinks was WINS, a top pop outlet, and its star prime-time jock, Murray the K, who, according to one competitor, was the heir to legendary DJ Alan Freed. The Beatles had met Murray in passing at the airport, a middle-aged leprechaun

with a massive personality and a magpie style that he referred to as his shtick. Murray was New York through and through. "He had a special affinity for street culture," says Daniel.

"I'm *Me-iz-Urray* the *Kee-zay!*" he'd shriek into the mike. "Cool as *abba-zawa*, baby!"

Murray was "as mad as a hatter," Ringo noted, "a fabulous guy, a great DJ, and he knew his music."

He also knew a golden opportunity when he saw one, and he mined the Beatles for all they were worth. Throughout their New York stay, Murray functioned as their personal promo man, lobbing them softballs and plugging their records. The Beatles played right along, dropping little publicity items like bread crumbs for Murray to follow. "We would give him all the exclusives because we loved him," Paul said. After spinning a half-dozen of their requests, Murray hollered, "This is the Beatles' station, baby! They've taken over! They're telling us what to play."

"One more week of this, and I'm going to become the fifth Beatle."—Murray the K

Early Friday night, George begged off from the ongoing repartee, bemoaning his evident lack of sleep. "I've been up for days," he apologized to Murray's radio audience, when in fact he was rapidly getting sick. It had begun to hit him on the plane ride over. At first he had complained of queasiness, which the boys dismissed as butterflies, but it progressed into a possible case of the flu. By Saturday morning, Feb. 8, there was no more uncertainty. His throat was raw; he could barely speak. When his temperature nudged past 102, a hotel doctor examined George and ordered him to bed.

It couldn't have come at a worse time. The Beatles were due at a morning press conference, followed by rehearsal for their three *Ed Sullivan* appearances. How did they expect to fill in for George? Not with the fifth Beatle, that was for sure. Instead, they recruited their road manager, Neil Aspinall, and prepared to hit the streets of New York.

Outside, the weather was blustery, the landscape bleached of essential color. Neither of which deterred the fans. The Beatles dodged a mob of bundled-up admirers, who shrieked at the sight of their shaggy-haired idols. Reporters scurried from one teenager to the next, attempting to capture any reasonable sound bite. "Elvis Presley's all right," a young woman told an interviewer, "but he's too old—he's old and ugly." Another girl, in a state of tearful hysteria, cried, "I touched Paul! I thought, 'Well, that's not going to be nothing.' *I touched Paul McCartney!* And I can't touch him again—ever again. *Never!*"

A thicket of blue-uniformed police, fighting to hold back the crowd, picked up limp, seemingly lifeless girls who had collapsed in delirium and slung them over shoulders to safety.

A few Juilliard music students eyed

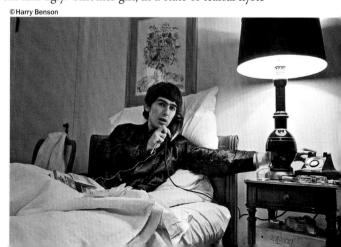

A CENTRAL PARK ZOO

Sans George, the boys hit the streets of New York. At the boathouse in the park, they mugged obediently for photographers and answered every dopey question with composure. The filmmaker Albert Maysles said, "For them, being in front of a camera meant performing for it."

the scene with palpable skepticism. "I just don't understand how people go crazy over four guys," said a young woman lugging an instrument case. "There are thousands just like them."

"I can play the guitar better," her friend chipped in, "and she can sing better."

But for the most part the reaction was rapturous. The highly charged crowd outside the Plaza was unusual even for New York. This wasn't quite Beatlemania, not pandemonium, not yet. But the sensation the boys caused, marked by screams and rampant hysteria, was an indicator of the uproar to come.

Unfazed by the attention, the Beatles, sans George, alighted at the boathouse in Central Park, where a pack of unruly paparazzi barked at them like animal trainers. "Hey, Beatles—*this* way!" they shouted. "Beatles—*this way*!" "No, not *this* way—the *other* way!"

Through it all, the Beatles mugged obediently and answered every dopey question. "What is your favorite food?" "What does your haircut mean?" "What do you think of American girls?" "How long do you think all this will last?"

Albert Maysles, who circled through the makeshift gathering, marveled at the boys' composure. "These guys, the Beatles, were almost from another planet," he observed. "For them, being in front of a camera meant performing for it. That had become their natural way of behaving."

But they could put up with the nonsense for only so long. During a break in the action, they jumped into an idling limo and instructed the driver to head uptown. They weren't particularly interested in the standard New York sights—the Empire State Building, the U.N., Rockefeller Center, the Statue of Liberty. Their destination was a more meaningful shrine. John wanted to "cruise past the Apollo Theater," Paul recalled, where so many of the Beatles' idols had debuted.

Unlike the vanilla-themed dregs of American pop, the early British guitar groups feasted on obscure R&B songs—flops and flip sides—to give weight to their set lists. It became something of a status symbol of northern English rockers to dig up an esoteric B-side that sounded original and suited their distinctive style: a heartfelt melody, chord patterns that repeated, exquisitely modulated phrasing and sudden downshifting into minor chords, lush Everly Brothers–style harmonies, all with a decidedly Mersey Beat twist. They could listen to something that was either raw or ignored and know instantly how to breathe new life into it.

Songs unheard of in America became standards in Liverpool, many courtesy of the early Beatles: "Anna" and "Soldier of Love" by Arthur Alexander, "Some Other Guy" by Richie Barrett, James Ray's "If You Gotta Make a Fool of Somebody," "Hippy Hippy Shake" by Chan Romero and "Devil in Her Heart" by the Donays, to name a few.

Later, of course, after the British rock scene exploded, beat groups retooled any number of neglected American gems into hits, such as "Go Now" (the Moody Blues via Bessie Banks), "Do Wah Diddy" (Manfred Mann via the Exciters), "I'm Into Something Good" (Herman's Hermits via Earl-Jean McCrea) and "Every Little Bit Hurts" (Spencer Davis via Brenda Holloway). But the Beatles, unlike many of their counterparts, endeavored to trace their musical roots, and a detour into Harlem seemed especially apropos.

There was little romance, however, in the Harlem that the Beatles encountered. A predomi-

They headed for Harlem, the source of so many of their musical influences. But they couldn't catch a performance at the storied Apollo Theater; there was no time to do more than drive past.

nantly African-American neighborhood that once jumped to the tempo of its bebop night world, it had lapsed by the early 1960s into an impoverished ghetto, its streets a warren of blighted tenements. Race relations in general were at an all-time low, and you could feel the residual backlash in Harlem's restless pulse. Everywhere there were people jostling on the sidewalk, spilling out of bodegas, jackknifing through traffic. Tension-filled faces, willful, unhappy.

The Beatles gaped at the bleak scenery as their limo cruised through the streets. The neighborhood was an eye-opener—threatening, grimy, alien, *exotic*. Not at all like in Liverpool, whose ghetto, the Dingle, was a bad-ass Irish enclave, but tidy and proud. Suddenly they turned onto a wide, jittery boulevard, 125th Street, and the Apollo loomed right in front of them. TONIGHT!—THE MARVELOUS MARVELETTES! read the marquee. *De-liveh de-letteh, de-sooneh de-betteh*: the girls themselves! So near—and yet so prohibitive, no thanks to the schedule.

The same with the specialty record shops that beckoned from every corner: salsa, soul, gospel, jazz, doo-wop, R&B, R&B, R&B. The Beatles, tempted by such offerings, had to restrain themselves from making innumerable stops. As it was, they barely made it back for the start of their *Ed Sullivan* rehearsal.

As they pulled up in front of the theater on Broadway, a less inviting scene awaited. John took a look out the car window and issued a one-word summary: "Kids."

Since early afternoon, the studio had come under siege as teenage fans thronged the entrance. Hundreds of onlookers lined the intersection.

"How are we gonna get in there?" Paul wondered.

Too late. Their car had been spotted by the frenzied horde.

"Lock the doors!" Ringo warned as a swarm of girls converged, screaming and banging on the windows in a staccato drumbeat.

Out of nowhere, a cordon of police on horseback pulled up alongside and gave the limo a critical escort to W. 53rd Street and the studio entrance.

"This it? Get in quick!" John insisted, as the Beatles piled out and made a dash for the studio's side entrance.

In the meantime, Brian Epstein spent most of Saturday dodging the hustlers who rang his hotel room. Every cheapjack in New York, it seemed, angled to pitch him a get-rich-quick

Epstein was a devoted manager, but he wasn't great at merchandising. He ignored opportunities for income from Beatles paraphernalia, which ranged from clocks, pillows and scarves to bobblehead dolls.

scheme hawking Beatles paraphernalia. All kinds of junk were already being produced to cash in—night-lights, clocks, sweaters, pillows, scarves, pens, bracelets, games and Beatles wigs galore—none of which put a dime in the band's pockets.

Merchandising wasn't exactly Epstein's long suit. In the five months since Beatlemania had taken hold, he'd all but ignored opportunities for ancillary income. It was like wildcatting: all anyone had to do was slap the name "Beatles" on a product and dump it on the market—no licenses required, no royalties paid, no questions asked. "Brian's made a terrible mess out of this," his lawyer, David Jacobs, told an eager entrepreneur attempting to tap the gusher.

Jacobs was engaged to stanch the financial hemorrhaging. Instead, he merely signed over the Beatles' merchandising rights to a slick-talking sharpie named Nicky Byrne for a 90–10 split, with Byrne pocketing the lion's share.

By the time Epstein arrived in New York, Byrne had strafed the American market under the corporate name Seltaeb—Beatles spelled backward—and was issuing licenses to manufacturing companies as if they were phony stock certificates. The *Wall Street Journal* predicted that "U.S. teen-agers in the next 12 months are going to spend $50 million on Beatle wigs, Beatle dolls, Beatle egg cups and Beatle T-shirts, sweatshirts and narrow-legged pants." Everywhere Epstein turned, he stumbled over another Nicky Byrne megadeal—and saw millions and millions of dollars go down the drain, with millions more at stake. This much he was sure of: if the Beatles ever found out, they'd make dog food out of him.

Epstein hadn't even met Byrne until Mr. Seltaeb appeared unannounced at the Plaza toting a sackful of gear he intended to man-

> WHAT A COLOSSAL ERROR BRIAN EPSTEIN HAD MADE. MILLIONS AND MILLIONS OF DOLLARS DOWN THE DRAIN, MILLIONS MORE AT STAKE. THIS MUCH HE WAS SURE OF: IF THE BEATLES EVER FOUND OUT, THEY'D MAKE DOG FOOD OUT OF HIM.

SCHOOL OF ROCK
Epstein and three-quarters of the
Beatles watch Ed Sullivan try out
Paul's Höfner violin bass (later dubbed
the Beatle bass) during a rehearsal
for Sullivan's Sunday-night show.

ufacture. Games, bobblehead dolls, shampoo, wallpaper. Beatles this, Beatles that ... Epstein took one look at the stuff and nearly had a stroke. On Saturday afternoon, negotiations to revise the deal promptly began.

The *Ed Sullivan* rehearsal was child's play by comparison. The show functioned as a smooth-running apparatus, in contrast with the many cheesy gigs the Beatles had played. Everyone—band members and network technicians alike—worked as a team to fine-tune the sound.

In the best of circumstances, miking a band was a nightmare, the sound levels so tricky to control. But a rock band? A hopeless case. Achieving an acceptable balance was akin to picking a lock. Until the Beatles, most teenage groups who appeared on that stage worked along with a house ensemble that included horns and strings. Not even self-contained bands such as the Everly Brothers were exempt from that extra padding. But Epstein had insisted: the Beatles played au naturel. They weren't just a bunch of hunks strumming guitars, like Ricky Nelson or Elvis. These boys could *play*; they were a force unto themselves. American TV audiences were going to get the full monty.

For their efforts, the Beatles won respect, and not only from the CBS stagehands. Capitol Records execs turned up backstage, full of cheer and flattery for their new star act. Nothing was said about the string of insults, the umpteen rejections, the "stone-cold dead in the U.S. marketplace." Those seemed like absurd jokes, considering the Beatles' hijacking of the American charts. Since the New Year, they had accounted for 60% of all record sales in the States. Go ahead, read that again: *60% of all record sales in the States.* Capitol's pressing plants were so overburdened by demand that the label outsourced production to RCA Victor's and Columbia's facilities for help in filling orders.

OH, WHAT A DIFFERENCE A MONTH MADE! Yes, all was forgotten, forgiven. In fact, Alan Livingston, the president of Capitol, was on his way personally from the Capitol Tower in L.A. to present the boys with two gold records. In the meantime, the label's East Coast honchos were at their disposal. Anywhere the Beatles wanted to go, anything they wanted to do—all they had to do was say the word. To show its appreciation, Capitol shoveled the boys into a limo for a first-class night on the town, beginning with a sightseeing tour around Manhattan, followed by dinner at "21," where Ringo ordered a bottle of "vintage Coca-Cola."

Saturday's events had proved demanding, stressful. The Beatles were exhausted when they arrived back at the Plaza. Nothing that a good night's rest wouldn't cure. But it was clear from the get-go that there would be no peace. TV news crews were camped out in the hall. Tom Wolfe was in their suite, taking notes for an *Esquire* article. Cynthia Lennon and George's sister, Louise, were entertaining a roomful of visitors. And plenty of others were reported to be on their way.

THE BEATLES HAD HAD IT WITH MURRAY THE K'S BARRAGE OF INANE ANTICS. AND WITH EVERYONE ELSE, FOR THAT MATTER, ESPECIALLY THE PHOTOGRAPHERS, THEIR CAMERAS CONTINUOUSLY SNAPPING LIKE CASTANETS. JOHN, WHO WAS CLEARLY ANNOYED, LAID DOWN THE LAW. "RONNIE, GET 'EM ALL OUT OF HERE," HE DEMANDED.

The Beatles were not happy. One name especially stood out. Murray the K, that notorious motormouth, was en route to interview George from his sickbed. Murray's request for an audience had already been denied, but he wouldn't take no for an answer. "He called my house and said, 'You gotta get me into the Plaza, honey,'" recalls Ronnie. Unable to refuse the powerful DJ, she headed to the hotel with a whole entourage, sparking a classic I'm-with-the-band moment, as Murray trailed the Ronettes into the Beatles' suite. But he soon wore out his welcome "asking dumb questions and making bad jokes about their hair."

The Beatles had had it with his barrage of inane antics. And with everyone else, for that matter, especially the photographers, their cameras continuously snapping like castanets. John, who was clearly annoyed, laid down the law. "Ronnie, get 'em all out of here," he demanded.

Even the effervescent Beatles needed their rest. They had a milestone moment ahead of them. Sunday was the most important performance of their career.

Ladies and Gentlemen...
THE BEATLES!

'A REALLY BIG SHEW'

The press swoops in during rehearsals for *The Ed Sullivan Show*. Though American audiences had yet to see the Beatles perform, the buzz surrounding their appearance was tremendous

If the Beatles were jittery about their *Ed Sullivan* appearance on Feb. 9, they didn't show it.

There wasn't a shred of anxiety about facing a national TV audience. They'd been through this before, in London and Manchester. Sure, the show was an American institution; every major celebrity put in an appearance: Frank Sinatra, Judy Garland, Nat King Cole, Elvis Presley. But the Beatles were as polished as any veteran performer. Nothing fazed them, whether 2,000 screaming girls or the queen of England.

The good news was that George was back on his feet, a bit wobbly but eager to get down to work. His temperature had fallen to a respectable level and his voice sounded fine, with none of the husk left in his throat. And in the nick of time. Without him, the Beatles weren't, well, the Beatles. The group was the sum of its integral parts. George's guitar served as the anchor to their arrangements. His tasty fills that unspooled between melody lines gave their songs a singular identity. And he could sing, not quite as stylishly as John and Paul, but with confidence, and his harmonies fattened the vocals.

The scene outside CBS's television studio was extraordinary, even for New York City. A troop of mounted police patrolled Broadway by the theater, where several thousand fans strained against

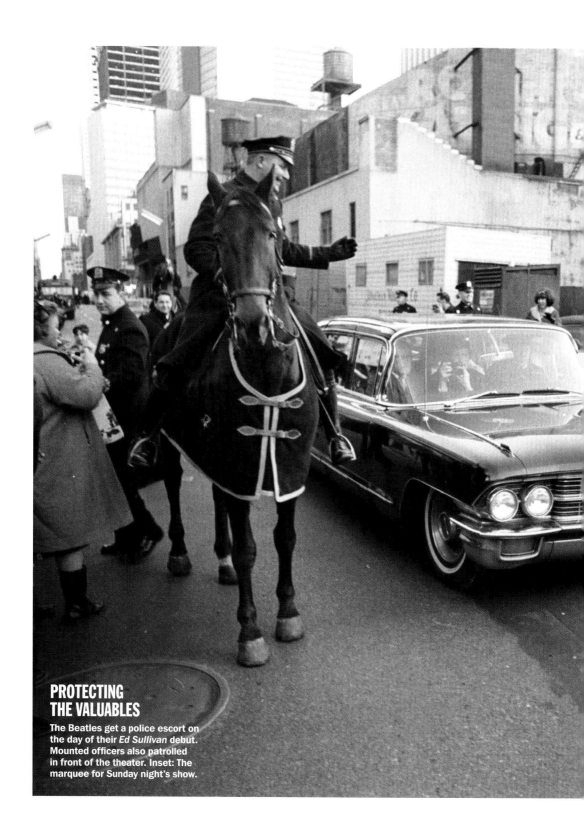

PROTECTING THE VALUABLES

The Beatles get a police escort on the day of their *Ed Sullivan* debut. Mounted officers also patrolled in front of the theater. Inset: The marquee for Sunday night's show.

barricades in an attempt to snag a precious seat. Every ticket had long been spoken for, but that didn't discourage the crowd. All afternoon it ballooned in size as fans confronted flustered gatekeepers in an effort to talk their way inside.

Normally this wouldn't have been an issue. As a rule, Sunday sound checks and rehearsals were conducted in an empty house to give technicians the chance to fine-tune details. But Sullivan, hoping to maximize his investment, had talked Brian Epstein into letting him tape an afternoon show, which he agreed to televise on Feb. 23, a day after the Beatles returned to London. So shortly after 9 a.m., the boys began the first of two full dress rehearsals, which brought the clamoring hordes to the theater by morning's first light.

In between run-throughs, John, Paul, George and Ringo lounged backstage, oblivious to the anticipation building outside. There was plenty of English tea and a stack of unopened telegrams from well-wishers across the country. One, with the word "Urgent" scrawled across the top in red ink, caught Paul's attention. As he read it, his face yielded a high-beam grin.

"It's from Elvis!" he shouted to the others.

John deadpanned, "Elvis who?"

Ignoring him, Paul read the cable aloud. "'Congratulations on your appearance on *The*

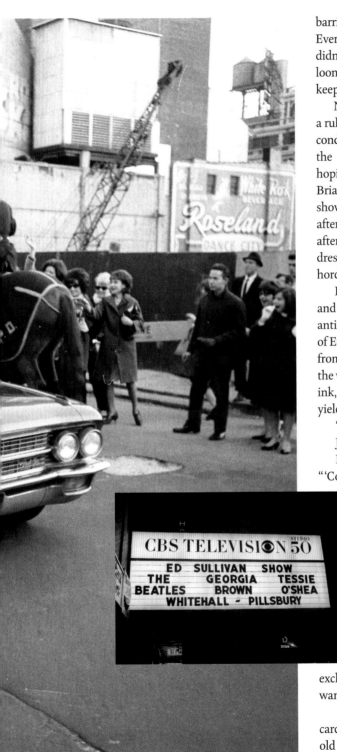

Ed Sullivan Show and your visit to America. We hope your engagement will be a successful one and your visit pleasant. Give our best to Ed Sullivan.'" He looked up, smiling. "'Sincerely, Elvis and the Colonel.'"

Just before 2:30, the Beatles got the signal to take their places. If they seemed daunted at making their American debut, it didn't show. They plugged in and waited patiently behind a curtain, exchanging relaxed, easy grins, as Ed Sullivan wandered onstage.

Sullivan was an improbable TV star. Stiff as cardboard and about as endearing, the 62-year-old emcee had, a profile in TIME said, as much charisma as "a cigar-store Indian." He was painfully awkward in front of the camera, but he had an uncanny instinct for spotting talent and the ability to give it a national showcase. As such, he was a powerful star maker, to say nothing of an American icon. If you tuned in on Sunday nights, as a majority of TV watchers did, you were in for "a really big shew."

Really big, but still a bastion of old-school entertainers—comedians like Jerry Lewis and Totie Fields, who came out of nightclubs like the Copacabana; Broadway-style crooners like Robert Goulet, who sang (and sang!) his signature "If Ever I Would Leave You"; endless acrobatic teams, ventriloquists and lovable puppets like the ever-present Topo Gigio. Sullivan's willingness to showcase something new, like the Beatles, would help topple the reign of his old mainstays.

The current big "shew" was a game changer. Even though American audiences had yet to see anything but TV news snippets of Beatles performances, the buzz was tremendous. Top 40 stations across the country had been plugging them all week by playing the records and talking up the visit, which had taken on prophetic significance. What was this British band all about? No one knew what to expect. The kids in Studio 50 could barely stay in their seats.

Sullivan must have known the high-pitched squeals weren't for him. As soon as he stepped in front of the curtain, the racket started, short bursts of girlish glee from the seats just beyond the footlights. The uproar increased as he thanked "these youngsters from Liverpool" and noted that they would "leave an imprint on everyone over here who's met them." By the time he said the magic words—"the Beatles"—you could barely hear him over the screams.

As the curtains parted, a grid of spotlights hit the boys, and the glow it cast has never dimmed. For the young audience, the Beatles were a sight to behold. With their handsome faces, seductive posture and outlandishly sculptured hair, they looked like a teenage fantasy come to life. For a split second, the audience stared awestruck. They'd seen Paul Anka, Frankie Avalon and Bobby Rydell, but these were beasts of a different nature. Not dangerous or unrefined, like Elvis. The boys projected a cool, postured image, hip, intense and unself-conscious all at once—the new face of rock 'n' roll.

The Beatles didn't waste any time in staking their claim to history. Standing center stage in their matching mohair-blend suits, they launched into a comparatively tame but rock-solid version of "Twist and Shout" that sent a visceral charge across the theater. "Shake it up, baby," indeed! John, who handled the lead, was in fine feisty voice, shredding the flourish at the end of each verse to give the delivery a raw, uneasy tug. Like clockwork, Paul and George collapsed around a single mike to provide the playful echo in the call-and-response, and when all three voices pounced on the "woooooo," they shook those famous haircuts in unison, a trick they had practiced on tour that was calibrated to wind up the crowd. Every time they did it, followed by sly, knowing grins, the mostly female audience howled on cue.

For all the commotion, the Beatles were unfaltering. Their act was edgy but polished. Above all, they knew how to work a room. Their showmanship, that mix of teenage aggression and those dazzling, seductive smiles, scored instantly with the kids.

At the end of the song, before anyone had a chance to cool off, the Beatles didn't lose a beat, ripping into "Please Please Me." The introduction alone hit a nerve, an exhilarating riff powered by George's crisp guitar picking that jacked up the temperature by more than a few degrees. You could feel the body heat shift in the audience. Especially when John and Paul leaned into their mikes and belted out those gorgeous harmonies. "Last night I said these words to *m-y-y-y g-i-r-r-r-l* ..." By the time they traded the "come on"s and pleaded their case—"Please *pleeeeeese* me, wo-yeah ..."—the place just went wild. Every girl thought they

IMAGE OF A NEW ROCK 'N' ROLL

Rehearsing for their Sunday performances, one of which would be televised two weeks later. They projected a cool, postured aura that was simultaneously hip, intense and unself-conscious.

were singing directly to her; every boy saw himself up there on that stage.

It was almost overkill when they segued into "I Want to Hold Your Hand." The record, released in America just six weeks earlier, was already a full-blown teenage anthem. As if the overheated arrangement weren't tantalizing enough, the Beatles' performance of it was extraordinary. From John and Paul's slashing harmonies to Paul's sudden full-octave leap into falsettoland, capped off by the inimitable "I can't *hide*, I can't *hide*," their delivery hit all the notes. In two and a half minutes, they'd put a torch to the American rock 'n' roll scene.

If the audience left the theater in ecstasy, the Beatles were anything but satisfied. "We weren't happy with the … appearance," said Paul, "because one of the mikes weren't [*sic*] working." John's vocals were muffled and often lost in the mix. It seemed incomprehensible to the boys, who were uncompromising when it came to sound. They'd worked painstakingly on it during rehearsals, listening to the playback after each take and helping the TV technicians adjust the levels until they were uniform and precise. "Finally," George recalled, "when they got a balance between the instruments and the vocals, they marked the boards by the controls, and then everyone broke for lunch. Then, when we came back to tape the show, the cleaners had been round and had polished all the marks off the board."

> **IF THE AFTERNOON AUDIENCE LEFT THE THEATER IN ECSTASY, THE BEATLES WEREN'T HAPPY. GEORGE LIT INTO SULLIVAN'S SON-IN-LAW, WHO PRODUCED THE SHOW. THE SOUND QUALITY, HE ARGUED, WAS UNACCEPTABLE.**

That evening, when the Beatles returned to Studio 50 for the live broadcast of *The Ed Sullivan Show*, George lit into Bob Precht, Sullivan's son-in-law, who produced the show. The sound quality, he argued, was unacceptable. This was too important a gig; the Beatles were leaving nothing to chance. In the midst of their heated exchange, visitors and dignitaries began streaming backstage to size up the four boys from Liverpool. Dizzy Gillespie, who was playing down the street at Birdland, "just stopped by to get a look at them," as did various Capitol Records execs and Carroll James, the WWDC disc jockey credited with introducing them to American listeners. The Beatles were already feeling pinched by the crowd. But when Leonard Bernstein swept in with his daughters, babbling about a visit to Washington and "singing rounds with Jackie [Kennedy] at breakfast," the boys had heard enough. John ordered the entire bunch chucked out and put the dressing room on lockdown.

As it was, the theater felt under siege. The crowd outside stretched over eight blocks, giving the place the revved-up energy of a Broadway opening. CBS had received more than 50,000 ticket requests; it seemed as though half that number were trying to get inside. Among those who did were Walter Cronkite's and Jack Paar's daughters, as well as Richard Nixon's 15-year-old daughter Julie. But seats were at a premium. Even Sullivan felt the pinch. On his show the week before, he had appealed to his audience. "Coincidentally," he said, "if anyone has a ticket for the Beatles on our show next Sunday, could I please borrow it? We need it very badly."

Backstage, the corridors had a rush-hour feel, with performers and technicians elbowing their way between dressing rooms and the wings. The show was always packed with acts, and this night was no exception. In addition to the Beatles, the bill included the comic team McCall and Brill; the impressionist Frank Gorshin; Wells & the Four Fays, the inevitable acrobats; the vaudevillian banjo player Tessie O'Shea; and stage star Georgia Brown, joined by the cast of the Broadway hit *Oliver!*, written by Lionel Bart, one of Brian Epstein's pals. In what had to be

EYE OF THE STORM

Backstage at the *Sullivan* show, there were plenty of well-wishers, idol worshippers and pranks. Left, from top: John photographs Paul; Walter Cronkite's daughters have their picture taken with the boys (the daughters of other famous people were in attendance too); George and his sister, Louise; Paul gets a mock haircut. Right, from top: Sullivan models a Beatles wig; Paul is interviewed; John takes a moment.

At the show on Sunday afternoon—the big one would come that night—their performance made clear that they weren't wasting any time in staking their claim to history.

ABOVE ALL, THEY KNEW HOW TO WORK A ROOM. THEIR SHOWMANSHIP, THAT MIX OF TEENAGE AGGRESSION AND THOSE DAZZLING, SEDUCTIVE SMILES, SCORED INSTANTLY WITH THE KIDS.

STAR MAKER AND STARS

Despite his cardboard-stiff personality, Sullivan was essential viewing for millions because of his uncanny eye for talent. Introducing the Beatles to America was one of his greatest triumphs in more than 20 years on television.

the worst billing of all time, magician Fred Kaps was scheduled to follow the Beatles.

"We were aware that Ed Sullivan *was the big one."*
—*George Harrison*

At 8 p.m. on Feb. 9, an unheard-of 60% of American TVs were tuned to CBS. The Beatles had caused a run on the airwaves that set all broadcast viewing records. Everyone wanted to have a look at the source of all that hoopla. How could four pop musicians—four boys from England—create so much excitement? It was beyond most American parents, who had watched the buildup with wary eyes. Their kids seemed to be under some kind of a spell, a Beatles spell, and they wanted to see what they were up against—beginning with that hair. "Dads invariably said, 'Those are wigs. They're wearing wigs!'" Paul recalled later. But that was just the tip of the iceberg. As far as most parents were concerned, the whole phenomenon was suspect—the accents, the look, the rock 'n' roll. They'd survived Elvis and they'd survive the Beatles, but rest assured they'd be in front of their TV sets, sitting right next to their kids, ready to hand down a clear-eyed verdict.

The audience in living rooms may have been split down the middle, but the makeup of the theater belonged to the Beatles. As the credits rolled, the camera scanned the audience: wall-to-wall teenagers, mostly girls who were wound a bit tight. Passionate female fans were a staple of pop heartthrobs, but this gang was something else, on the edge of frenzy.

Sullivan didn't give them time to steal the thunder. "Now, yesterday and today, our theater's been jammed with newsmen and hundreds of photographers from all over the nation," he said, "and these veterans agree with me that the city's never witnessed the excitement stirred by these youngsters from Liverpool who call themselves the Beatles." A smattering of screams churned through the audience. "Now, tonight, you're gonna twice be entertained by them, right now and

SINGING DIRECTLY TO THEM

The audiences were packed with row after row of teenage girls. Passionate female fans were a staple of pop heartthrobs, but these crowds were on the edge of frenzy.

in the second half of the show. Ladies and gentlemen … *the Beatles!*"

At last! The curtains swept open and America had its first look at the band—not in black leather and stagy scowls, not intimidating, as some had feared, but neatly groomed, all smiles, vaguely harmless: a pleasant surprise. *The Beatles!* Without hesitation, they launched right into a crisp if workmanlike version of "All My Loving," a cut from their freshly minted LP, *Meet the Beatles*, which topped *Billboard*'s charts the following week and remained there until it was knocked off by their second album. Paul sang it note-perfect, but with all the delicious fat siphoned off, as though he'd decided to homogenize it for general consumption. The song hummed along nicely, breaking for a laid-back, twangy guitar riff that George handled with flair, punctuated by Ringo's steady backbeat. Still, the Beatles' magic was cheated by the sound demons. John's mike was muddy, burying his vocals, so that the overall balance was lopsided and indistinct.

After taking a gracious bow at the end, Paul soloed on "Till There Was You."

The song, a highlight from Broadway's *The Music Man*, was an unorthodox choice for the Beatles' debut, the kind of corny standard that young British bands sprinkled through their sets as concessions to the naysayers of rock 'n' roll. And Paul sang it so sweetly, oozing sincerity. Paul was loaded with boyish charm, which he'd perfected as an art form, and he played it for all it was worth, staring into the camera and projecting the most innocent, adorable image that American girls had ever witnessed. Young hearts melted when he flipped that particular switch.

More than a few eyes widened, though, as the camera lingered on each of the Beatles' faces and a crawl appeared at the bottom of the screen, identifying them by name. Paul McCartney, doe-eyed; George Harrison, jug-eared and stoic; Ringo Starr, grinning earnestly. When John Lennon got his close-up at the very end, an unexpected postscript revealed, "Sorry, girls, he's married." That let a big cat out of the bag. Until that moment,

John's marriage had been not only hush-hush but hotly denied by the Beatles' management. Epstein had decided early on that the presence of a girlfriend—and especially a wife—would turn off the female fans. As such, Cynthia Lennon was forced to deny her marriage, even her name, to anyone who asked. She kept a low profile, never wore a wedding band, learned how to blend into the crowd. At shows, John would often stash her at the back of the hall, where she would watch like any other desperate fan. Moreover, they carefully avoided going out together in public.

For almost two years the British press had played along, plying a cozy, if irresponsible, relationship with the band. Incredibly, when the Beatles asked that a personal matter not be revealed, reporters complied. A wanton tabloid mentality had not yet taken hold. In fact, during an interview that Judith Simons of the *Daily Express* conducted with the boys in the fall of 1963, she said, "We still can't mention your marriage, can we, John?" And she didn't.

A secret held by a willing press for almost two years is finally revealed.

"I like to keep my work and my private life separate," John said at the time, "which is why I keep Cynthia out of the picture." But "I took her to America, because a trip like that comes once in a lifetime, and she deserved it." Now there was acknowledgment that John was married, and so be it, damn the consequences.

If news of John's marriage sucked the energy out of the performance for a few lovestruck fans, the boys quickly sent them airborne again. The moment the ballad closed with George's little cha-cha flourish on the guitar, Paul jerked sideways on a heel and whipped his finger around a few times to launch Ringo into gear. A clatter of drums erupted into "She Loves You," jolting the audience. The song had a tremendous, explosive energy that burst from the opening notes into a beautiful split of harmonies. This was the groove the audience had been waiting for; it grabbed them from the get-go. When the band hit the "woooo"s at the end of the chorus, Paul and John exaggerated the shake of their heads, which triggered shrieks of delight.

THE LAST TWO NUMBERS were even more riveting. Both "I Saw Her Standing There" and "I Want to Hold Your Hand" delivered on the promise of something thrilling. The boys kicked into overdrive, wringing every last ounce of juice from the songs that revitalized and transformed the medium of rock 'n' roll. Each lasting under two and a half minutes, they packed a lifelong wallop. The songs were so alive, so accessible, so stylized. The whole package was intact and inspired: the arrangements jumped with boundless energy, the singing was full of exuberance, the performances sharp, flawless, laced with charm and personality. The impact was huge. As the camera cut to the crowd, there were glimpses of budding Beatlemania—row after row of young girls in the grip of ecstasy, their faces flushed, churning in their seats. It was a completely new and alien sensation. Yet all in all, the reaction was fairly restrained in contrast to the pandemonium evidenced overseas. No one sobbed, fainted or tried to leap onto the stage. For that matter, no one left her seat. It was a rather well-disciplined group of kids—perhaps the last of its kind at any Beatles performance.

The phenomenon unfolded in living rooms across the country. According to the A.C. Nielsen Co., the viewing audience was estimated at about 74 million people, reflecting a total of 23.24 million homes, a record for any TV show. Entire families were drawn to the Beatles' performance for personal, if disparate, reasons. It was a generational encounter: us against them. Adults weren't just skeptical about the Beatles' merit, musical or otherwise—they were prepared for a fight. No long-haired hooligans were going to undermine their values. But parents found something totally different from what they'd expected. The Beatles, as it turned out, were irresistible. They were sweet, not threatening, and what's more, they could sing.

The famous generation gap that would define the 1960s had yet to solidify. Here were kids watching their new idols on an old-fashioned show that featured their parents' favorites. And here were the parents, waiting for Tessie O'Shea to come on but keeping an open mind to see what this new phenomenon might be. The kids had not yet staked their claim to the culture. No lines had been drawn that people weren't willing to cross. That would come later, but for now the family television set had become a safe place to see what the other side was up to.

Ronnie Spector remembers watching the performance with her mother and fighting an undisciplined rush of nerves. "My mom and I gathered around the set in our apartment, and I could barely stay in my seat," she recalls. "It seemed so important to me that the Beatles do well, not just for their sakes but for something much larger, something unclear. I couldn't put my finger on it at the time, but I knew there was something significant at stake."

Something—wonderful and unexplainable. No one had seen anything like it before.

"To me, they were four parts of one person, and that person was me," Jann Wenner told TIME, referring to the life-altering event that took place three years before he founded *Rolling Stone*. "For me, it was their joy more than anything—their happiness. I wanted to be like the Beatles, having so much fun."

In Hicksville, N.Y., a 14-year-old boy named Billy Joel had to run down the street to his friend Greg's house in time to catch the show. "My family didn't have a TV set," Joel told TIME recently, recalling that evening with clarity undiminished by 50 years. "I think I'd heard 'I Want to Hold Your Hand' on Murray the K's program. Otherwise I didn't know too much about [the Beatles]. But there was a lot of buzz. Like everybody else, I wanted to see what they were about."

The experience got off to a rocky start. "It was in black and white," Joel recalled, "not the best reception, a grainy picture. We had to play with the antenna."

Joel, who had been taking classical piano lessons for about 10 years, "blocked out everything" around him and watched the Beatles intently, feeling for the first time the emotional tug of rock 'n' roll. "It was a watershed moment in my life," he said. "I could tell right away they weren't manufactured in Hollywood. They were the real deal, exciting, perfectly balanced—it spoke right to me. It turned me inside out."

Billy Joel wasn't alone in this epiphany. Teenagers of all shapes and stripes were intoxicated. The Beatles communicated in ways both powerful and convincing, connecting teenagers to something that confirmed their adolescent impulses. They gave rock 'n' roll a new sound—and a new look. The nerve they struck with an American audience had immediate and extraordinary consequences.

"I watched them that night and said, 'That's what I want to do,'" Joel said. "The next day I was in a rock 'n' roll band."

A 14-YEAR-OLD BILLY JOEL WATCHED THE SHOW ON TV. "IT WAS A WATERSHED MOMENT IN MY LIFE," HE SAID. "THE NEXT DAY I WAS IN A ROCK 'N' ROLL BAND."

BRUISED BUT NOT BEATEN

The critics were harsh about their TV performance. Downbeat as they faced a news conference the next day, the Beatles would manage to rally their high spirits and charm the press all over again.

Pans and Pandemonium

The reviews of the Beatles' *Ed Sullivan* appearance brought everything back down to earth.

The boys paged through a stack of them with feigned indifference early the next morning, Feb. 10, over breakfast in their Plaza suite. The table was strewn with dailies that featured their TV debut prominently. They were delighted at first by the extent of coverage, but their faces soon collapsed into furrows and wrinkled brows reflecting the off-key tone of the criticism.

It seemed no one of note had appreciated their act. "Televised Beatlemania," wrote the *New York Times* TV critic, "appeared to be a fine mass placebo," and he dismissed the Beatles as nothing more than a "fad." The way he saw it, the performance itself was a "sedate anticlimax" to all the ballyhoo since the boys had hit town. Rather than trying to judge their artistry, he deferred to a highbrow colleague, who evaluated the music as one might a New York Philharmonic production, citing the Beatles' tendency to create "false modal frames … suggesting the Mixolydian mode."

The *Herald Tribune*, while less convoluted, gave it a page-one treatment under the puzzling banner BEATLES BOMB ON TV. Its columnist blasted the absence of talent in their performance, calling it "a magic act that owed less to Britain than

Photo by Henry Grossman, ©2012 Grossman Enterprises LLC

to Barnum." The Beatles "apparently could not carry a tune across the Atlantic," he wrote, rating the overall appearance as "75 percent publicity, 20 percent haircut, and 5 percent lilting lament."

And it went downhill from there. The *Washington Post* thought they "seemed downright conservative ... asexual and homely." And its sister publication, *Newsweek*, pulled out all the literary artillery for its scathing review:

"Visually they are a nightmare: tight, dandified Edwardian beatnik suits and great pudding bowls of hair. Musically they are a near-disaster, guitars and drums slamming out a merciless beat that does away with secondary rhythms, harmony and melody. Their lyrics (punctuated by nutty shouts of yeah, yeah, yeah!) are a catastrophe, a preposterous farrago of Valentine-card romantic sentiments."

Even Walter Cronkite, one of the few TV newscasters to have been granted an exclusive Saturday-night interview, was unable to conceal his distaste. "I was appalled by the music, which did not appeal to me at all," he confessed much later. "The appearance of the young men offended me. The long hair was only down over the tops of their ears, but it was still a radical departure from the haircuts most men favored in those days."

Publicly, the Beatles brushed off such criticism. "If everybody really liked us, it would be a bore," John said diplomatically to a reporter later that day. "It doesn't give any edge to it if everybody just falls flat on their face saying, 'You're

Newsweek

Bugs About Beatles

"VISUALLY THEY ARE A NIGHTMARE: TIGHT, DANDIFIED EDWARDIAN BEATNIK SUITS AND GREAT PUDDING BOWLS OF HAIR. MUSICALLY THEY ARE A NEAR-DISASTER ..."

THE MIDAS TOUCH

Alan Livingston, president of their American label, Capitol, presents the band with gold records for the single of "I Want to Hold Your Hand" and the album *Meet the Beatles*.

MAKE MINE MANHATTAN
The Peppermint Lounge, New York's hottest
club of the day, was reminiscent of the
Cavern in Liverpool. Inset: Ringo danced
with a succession of women till closing time.

great.'" But privately George fumed, especially over the Barnum comment, calling the crack "fucking soft."

Perhaps no one took criticism of the Beatles harder than Brian Epstein. To him it was personal, and he was hopping mad, lashing out at the reviews as a "vicious attack." He was already peeved by America's early dismissal of the boys, but this latest slight seemed to refuel his wrath.

Throwing a tantrum in his suite, he canceled the remainder of the band's interviews on the schedule, though he later reconsidered after his frazzled press officer intervened.

Just in time, too, because the boys were facing a daylong marathon of news conferences that drew an impressive crowd of leading journalists. By now, everyone knew what great copy the Beatles made, which brought out the press corps, pens poised and cameras pointed. The reviews may have been crummy, but the ratings prevailed. The Beatles were an out-and-out media sensation.

Even so, irritation with the reporters burned clearly on Epstein's face as he led the boys single file into their first conference in the Terrace Room. The turnout did nothing to soothe his pique, and he splintered off from them into a corner, smoldering, arms clasped tightly around his sides as if to restrain himself from striking anyone. A Capitol Records official observing the scene noted the warp in Brian's posture. "Before Epstein came here he had ice water in his veins," he said. "Now it's turned to vinegar."

NO MATTER—THE BEATLES CHARMED THE CROWD with their usual aplomb. The official purpose of this conference was to announce their three-picture deal with United Artists, which had been consummated in London shortly before they left, but the Beatles played it strictly for laughs. Without waiting to be asked, John announced, smirking, that his choice for a leading lady was Brigitte Bardot.

"How about you, Ringo?" someone called out.

"I don't mind, meself," he said, "as long as it's not Sophia Loren. She's so tall. I'd have to climb a ladder to kiss her!"

A reenergized Ringo smiled broadly at his audience. He was having the time of his life in New York, where, for some strange reason, his popularity eclipsed that of his more tantalizing bandmates. "When we got to America," he observed, "it wasn't *John, Paul, George* and Ringo. Half the time it was *Ringo, Paul, George* and *John* ... Suddenly it was equal."

But John continued to steal the spotlight. When asked to comment on the *Times*'s charge of creating "false modal frames," he snapped, "We're gonna see a doctor about that."

From across the room a woman asked George, "Who chooses your clothes?"

"We choose our own," John said. "Who chooses yours?"

"My husband," she answered. "Now tell me, are there any subjects you prefer not to discuss?"

John leaned in close to the microphone and grinned, saying, "Yes, your husband."

Appreciative laughter thundered throughout the room.

Despite the snarky criticism, the Beatles relished fencing with the press, trading the kind of sharp-edged wisecracks and one-liners that seemed polished by comedy writers. They were naturals. Their gift for firing off a comeback was masterful. They made it look effortless. John, in particular, flashed an irreverent tongue. A disciple of the offbeat humor and double-talk of the Goons, a beloved British comedy ensemble featuring Spike Milligan, Peter Sellers and Harry Secombe, he'd studiously imitated their timing and wit. It had rubbed off on Paul, George and Ringo as well. "That's the way we do everything," John explained, "everything's tongue in cheek. We're the same about ourselves, we never take it seriously." They kept up the relentless pace throughout the afternoon conferences, giving as good as they got, never once buckling under the strain. The result was a public-relations sensation. The Beatles' drollery defanged the hard-core press; their gung-ho spirit, their willingness to play ball gave them immunity.

"We'd learnt the whole game. We knew how to handle the press when we arrived. The British press are the toughest in the world—we could handle anything." —John Lennon

THE THIRD PRESS OUTING OFFERED a welcome break from the exhaustive volleys: Alan Livingston, president of Capitol Records, stepped forward to present the boys with two gold records, by which time the Beatles had expunged any whiff of the reviews.

For much of the band's New York visit, the press rarely strayed from their sides, tagging along wherever they went in the hope of snagging a quotable comment. The night before, a cordon of reporters had flanked their arrival at the Peppermint Lounge. At the time, the W. 45th Street disco was the hottest nightspot in New York, a go-go celebrity hangout with its own No. 1 hit song, "The Peppermint Twist," by its irrepressible house band, Joey Dee and the Starliters (who eventually morphed into the Young Rascals). Unlike most cavernous clubs that catered to dance crowds, the Pep, as it was called, was a broom closet whose capacity was limited to 178 people, and that included the barflies, four deep, at the mahogany counter along the wall. The place was claustrophobic—insufferably hot, loud, smoky, *rocking*—much like the Cavern in Liverpool. The dance floor, so to speak, was a postage-stamp-size piece of property in the back, where Ringo frugged endlessly until closing time with a series of attractive women. Ringo was an expert dancer, light and nimble on his feet and an unabashed extrovert, unlike his fellow Beatles, who mostly sat out the action. In fact, John and Paul were notorious clodhoppers, a symptom that can be linked to the charge that their songs, for the most part, cannot be danced to.

That didn't stop them from reveling in the scene. It was a far cry from the more buttoned-down atmosphere in London, which wouldn't officially "swing" for another two years. New York functioned as a pulsating all-night city, and "the Beatles couldn't get enough of it," according to a colleague. Then again, they were grateful to escape their Plaza suite, no longer prisoners of their skyrocketing fame.

On Feb. 11, the day after their Plaza press extravaganza, they really started to mix it up with the natives. They were due to give an evening performance in Washington, D.C., their first concert in America. Plans had been made to fly into the capital, but a flash snowstorm early that morning crippled the New York airports, forcing a last-minute change. It was decided to transport them by train instead. A private sleeping car was chartered expressly for the trip, not the glamorous Orient Express–style accommodations that such a conveyance might suggest but a tatty vintage boxcar, stale from cigarette smoke and outfitted with bench seats whose springs had seen better days. Neither glamorous nor private: what seemed like most of the New York press corps pushed into the car along with the Beatles. There was nowhere

The boys had no privacy on the train during their D.C. trip but took it in stride. Clockwise from top: The relentless press; the Lennons (Cynthia is disguised in a dark wig); Ringo makes friends with a conductor.

for the boys to hide. For nearly four hours, as the train chugged south, they were at the mercy of anyone who imposed. But the Beatles took it all in stride. They chatted and mingled at their uproarious best, so different from the way stars are now—distant, with their army of handlers. John and Paul sauntered through the train, interacting with the paying passengers and posing for pictures.

Considering the significance of their upcoming gig, the Beatles were particularly relaxed. It wasn't until the train pulled into Union Station that the impact of the event hit them. DJs had put the word out that the Beatles were arriving by rail, and an estimated 3,000 kids thronged the platforms, awaiting their car. At first the unruly crowd made it impossible for them to dis-

In snow-covered Washington for their Coliseum concert, they were asked whether they or the storm would have more effect. John: "The snow will probably last longer." Ringo: "Yeah, we're going tomorrow."

embark. Fans and local press battled for position, pushing and elbowing toward the train, amid a cascade of popping flashbulbs. There was complete chaos. The police, who were unprepared and outmanned, took cover on the sidelines as Paul led the entourage gamely toward the exits. Improbable as it seemed, the Beatles were used to such scenes and had suitable escape strategies in their playbook—they could get out of quicksand if necessary. Somehow they threaded their way through the snarl into getaway limos idling at the station's entrance.

D.C.'s cavalcade of well-lit monuments entertained the four Beatles as they made their way

toward the Washington Coliseum. It was an enormous redbrick building in the heart of the city, an outdated arena that no longer hosted prestigious events, first catering to ice hockey, then basketball and, later, boxing. Still, it was the largest venue they'd ever played—with the promoter jamming 2,500 temporary seats up to the lip of the stage to accommodate 8,100 fans. The boxing-match layout dictated that the Beatles would perform in the round, meaning on a central platform with the audience on all sides. To satisfy the fans, they'd have to shift positions and move the equipment after every few songs, an arrangement that pleased no one. In any case, it promised to be an adventure.

As incredible as it sounds, the Beatles' shows rarely lasted more than a half hour, so three opening acts warmed up the crowd. American teen idol Tommy Roe had been part of their first U.K. tour a year earlier, and the lads were delighted to see him again, if only to taunt him about the cash they'd relieved him of in payday poker games. They also intended to catch a set by the Chiffons (whose hit "He's So Fine" would later get George into hot water when they successfully sued him for pinching the melody to use in "My Sweet Lord"), but they had to scrap their plans when Murray the K shuffled backstage with his gear to broadcast live from their dressing room. Murray's "fifth Beatle" shtick was fast growing old. He'd become a pain in the ass since that first day in New York, camping outside their hotel suite on a nightly basis. It was getting harder for the Beatles to shake him, which made it something of a relief when it was time to hit the stage.

Theaters in the round were hardly a new phenomenon. They'd been around since ancient Greece and provided for real intimacy, removing the so-called fourth wall, thereby bringing

Gathering candy at the Coliseum. In Britain, Beatles fans threw Jelly Babies onto the stage. But those candies were soft; the jelly beans that the D.C. audience lobbed were, said George, like "little bullets."

the actors into the same space as the audience. In such situations the performers entered through tunnels under the stage. That would have made life easy for the Beatles. But this place wasn't laid out that way. "Because it was an ice rink, there was no way to come up from under the stage," recalled Carroll James, the Washington disc jockey, who was on hand for the show. The problem was serious: How could security get the Beatles onstage without sending them through a gauntlet of screaming kids? James, who was standing backstage, got tapped for duty by Harry Lynn, the show's promoter. "Your job is to keep everybody diverted," Lynn instructed him. So James, along with two fellow jocks, donned Beatles wigs and ran suicidally through the crowd, while the band, flanked by 40 ushers, charged down another aisle and sprinted up a few steps onto the stage.

THE ARENA FELT AS IF IT WERE UNDER ATTACK. An explosion of flashbulbs lit up the place and was amplified by a surge of surrounding screams that shook the creaky foundation. The sound built steadily to a deafening climax. "The reaction was so overwhelming," Paul recounted backstage after the show, calling it "the most tremendous reception I have ever heard in my life."

The crowd's high-tension response pumped up the Beatles. They knew from experience playing violent clubs in Liverpool and Hamburg not to let much downtime elapse, lest the boredom lead to punch-ups.

"Hello, hello, hello!" Paul screamed into the mike, performing a quick sound check while Ringo saddled up behind his drum kit and his mates quickly plugged in and got into position.

From where they stood, the situation looked perilous. There were no barriers between them and the audience. Fans practically spilled onto the stage. And the setup looked like an

THE MAIN EVENT

With the boxing-match layout, there were no barriers between them and the audience—on any side. Urged on by the fight-crowd atmosphere, they played with jacked-up intensity, the volume cranked as high as possible.

WITH THE BEATLES
RARE DISCOVERY

Photographer: Mike Mitchell

For weeks, 18-year-old Mike Mitchell felt growing excitement about the British boy band that was coming to the Coliseum in Washington, D.C., on Feb. 11, 1964. Just out of high school, working as a freelance photographer, Mitchell wangled a press pass from the now-defunct *Washington* magazine that put him at the lip of the stage. "I didn't want to document the concert," he recalls. "I wanted to create intimate portraits that showed who these alien beings were." He even scrambled onstage during the pre-concert press conference to snap dozens of shots within just a few feet of John, Paul, George and Ringo. "I was waiting for someone to tell me I couldn't be there, but nobody said a word." The fact that he couldn't afford a flash for his Nikon forced him to work with available lighting, which gave his close-ups an ethereal, iconic quality. Mitchell eventually piled the night's take into a storage box where it remained nearly forgotten until 2007, when he started to run out of money and eventually lost his home. With the help of a couple of friends and a local collector, he brought 46 restored images to Christie's New York City auction house, which dubbed the collection "The Beatles Illuminated: The Discovered Works of Mike Mitchell." In 2011—47 years after they were tucked away in a dark, dusty basement—the fruits of Mitchell's boyhood efforts burst into the light, fetching a whopping $362,000. (A buyer purchased the backlit photo on our contents page for $68,500.) Mitchell's dedication to fine-art photography continues, but now, he says, "I can breathe."

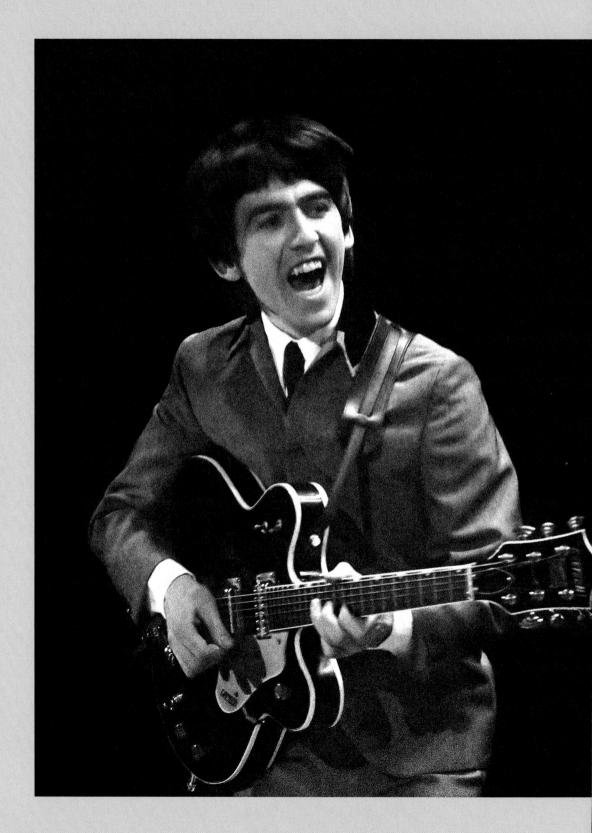

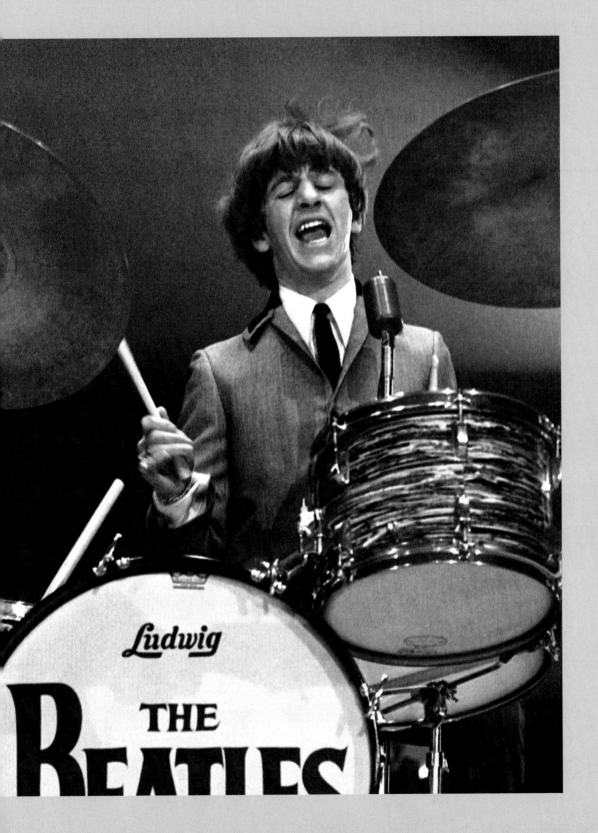

obstacle course, what with the tangle of arms reaching toward them, a maze of black cables snaking across the platform, and the sound equipment perched precariously atop makeshift plinths. "The acoustics were terrible," George recalled. This was the Pleistocene era when it came to stagecraft. There were no monitors, no sound board, no mixers, no follow spots. Paul, John and George were plugged into modest-size amps and speakers; as far as equipment went, that was it.

Like alchemists, the Beatles turned the misfortune into energy. From the opening bars of "Roll Over Beethoven," they let it rip, harnessing the elements of chaos around them into a powerhouse performance, a selection of all-out rockers with the volume cranked as high as possible, urged on by the fight-crowd atmosphere. They played with a jacked-up intensity that went far beyond their usual airtight set. "Ringo, in particular, played like a madman," wrote the biographer Albert Goldman. Something primitive had taken hold of him. His arms flailed ferociously and his head shook with demonic resolve, bombarding the arena with a propulsive backbeat. From the seats it sounded like enemy fire, only no one bothered to take cover. The kids threw themselves wholeheartedly into the spectacle. For most of them, this was the first experience of the overwhelming power of rock 'n' roll, and they abandoned all social proprieties to base emotion. "All the Beatlemania elements are here in Washington," the British rock paper *NME* reported.

"What an audience! I could have played for them all night," Ringo gushed backstage afterward, drenched in sweat. "They could have ripped me apart and I wouldn't have cared."

By the finale—Paul's convulsive, near-feral rendition of "Long Tall Sally"—the capacity crowd was on its feet, screaming uncontrollably in one mad, sustained roar.

FOR A FIRST LIVE AMERICAN SHOW, it was nothing short of a smash. The Beatles left the Coliseum elated—but wounded nonetheless, nursing a speckling of welts from airborne jelly beans. During an interview in England, George had casually mentioned that he liked eating Jelly Babies, the soft, squishy candies wrapped in cellophane, and fans there started the practice of throwing them onstage at shows. Something, however, got lost in the translation. The kids in Washington interpreted the term to mean jelly beans, with their hard outer shell. "That night, we were absolutely pelted by the fucking things," George recalled. "To make matters worse, we were on a circular stage, so they hit us from all sides. Every now and again, one would hit a string on my guitar and plonk off a bad note as I was trying to play."

Otherwise, the Beatles were in a celebratory mood, and a good thing, too, because Epstein had arranged for them to attend a little after-concert gathering in their honor at the British embassy just outside Georgetown. As a rule, they avoided these kinds of functions. "We always try to get out of those crap things," especially minutes after finishing a show, George said. But Epstein had assured them it would be a quiet little party for the overworked staff; an appearance by the Beatles would lift their home pride. In effect, said Ringo, the boys had "suddenly become ambassadors," which seemed like a worthy enough role.

As the car pulled up to the entrance, however, they could tell instantly that they'd been had. The building, said George Martin, was crawling with people in fancy dress, the "full quota of chinless wonders"—women in designer gowns, men in black tie, a diplomatic receiving line, a very la-di-da affair. More specifically, a "champagne party and masked charity ball," as stated on the embossed invitations. The Beatles were greeted with pomp by the British ambassador,

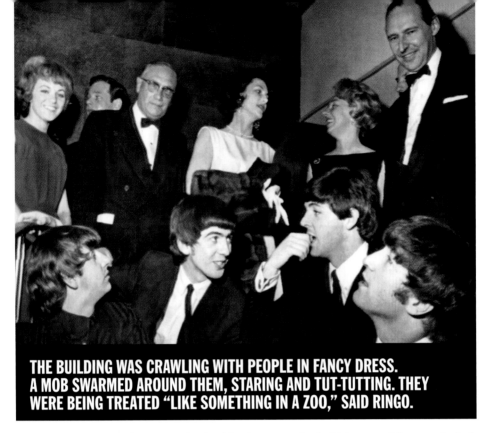

THE BUILDING WAS CRAWLING WITH PEOPLE IN FANCY DRESS. A MOB SWARMED AROUND THEM, STARING AND TUT-TUTTING. THEY WERE BEING TREATED "LIKE SOMETHING IN A ZOO," SAID RINGO.

David Ormsby-Gore, who managed a chuckle when Ringo looked him up and down and asked, "So what do you do?"

None of the Beatles was pleased by the situation. An aggressive mob swarmed around them, staring and tut-tutting. It felt as though they were on exhibit, "like something in a zoo," Ringo observed. John's nose was particularly out of joint. "People were touching us when we walked past," he complained. Ringo, sensing his irritation, talked John out of making a scene, but it was difficult to keep up the pleasantries. When a "slightly drunk woman" cornered Paul and demanded to know his name, Paul replied, "Roger. Roger McClusky the Fifth," before escaping from her clutches.

Somehow the boys got roped into announcing the winner of a raffle. They cooperated, albeit reluctantly, but during the exchange a young woman sneaked up behind Ringo and lopped off a hank of his hair with nail scissors. It was the final straw. "What the hell do you think you are doing?" he growled, furious at the breach of etiquette.

A guest near him said, chuckling, "Oh, it's OK, old chap." But Ringo was not to be assuaged. "Bullshit—bullshit," he fumed. "This lot here are terrifying—much worse than the kids."

John, who had observed the incident, stormed out of the ballroom, swearing under his breath. The other Beatles followed closely on his heels.

Harry Benson, the British photographer who was part of their entourage, said, "They were very sad. They looked as if they wanted to cry. They weren't pugnacious. They were humiliated."

Until now they had always played ball, doing whatever was asked of them, even if it seemed cockamamie or buffoonish. Saying hello to Lord So-and-So, mugging for the cameras, politely answering any question, no matter how ridiculous or condescending. It was part of the game, they figured, good for their careers. But no longer. That night had finished it for good. There was only so much rudeness they would endure. Sure, they were the Beatles; they knew their role. But they wouldn't play that part again, not with people like that. Not ever.

CAN'T GET ENOUGH

Fans at New York's Penn Station awaiting their idols' return. In an effort to avoid hysteria, cops detached the Beatles' train car and sent it to an isolated platform. The boys escaped into a taxi.

Get Back

The unrelenting spotlight and grueling schedule were starting to wear on the Beatles.

The constant encroachment and the extraneous obligations were exhausting. In the space of a few days, they'd ceded any illusion of privacy—to Murray the K, to the embassy stuffed shirts and especially to the news media. There were none of the boundaries they were used to in England.

On the morning of Feb. 12 they were put on a slow-moving train rattling up the East Coast, while Brian Epstein and his staff flew the shuttle back to New York. The boys, for their part, were chaperoned by an entourage of journalists who refused to give them a moment's peace. No matter how hard the Beatles tried to discourage conversation, there was no letup from the non-stop questions, the unending clicking of camera shutters, the chorus hounding them to "be a good sport." George Martin described the experience as "some giant three-ring circus," with the Beatles as stand-ins for the trained seals. Still, they got a bit of relief. George Harrison, fighting off the remnants of his illness, climbed into the overhead luggage rack and managed to steal a few winks. And Ringo comically swept out the car with a broom before collecting camera cases from the press photographers, stringing them around his neck, then shuffling up and down the aisle, shouting, "Exclusive *Life* magazine! Exclu-

LOVE WILL FIND A WAY

Officers attempt to restrain some passionate fans. The size of the welcoming crowds caught the police off guard, making their feeble attempts at security useless.

sive! I have a camera!" "We enjoyed it in the early days," George recalled, but "the only place we ever got any peace was when we got in the suite and locked ourselves in the bathroom."

But that wasn't about to happen anytime soon. The platforms were mobbed with several thousand fans when the train pulled into Pennsylvania Station. In order to clear the rabble from in front of the Plaza Hotel, the police had unwittingly put the word out that the Beatles would be heading straight to Carnegie Hall from the train, which set off a mass migration to greet the boys at the station. Barricades were hastily thrown up to cordon off the kids, but—nothing doing. Such an enormous crowd had caught the transit police off guard, making their feeble attempts at security useless.

At the last minute, the cops detached the Beatles' car from the rest of the train and diverted it to an isolated platform. A plan to take them up a special elevator was foiled by fans, so the boys charged up the closest set of stairs and jumped into a taxi idling on Seventh Avenue. They were overdue for rehearsal at Carnegie Hall, where they were scheduled to appear twice that evening.

Even for the Beatles, Carnegie Hall was no ordinary gig. The place was a shrine; the name alone humbled any musician. *How do you get to Carnegie Hall? Practice, practice, practice*—it was more than just a cornball joke. Carnegie Hall was the ultimate stage. It was where Tchaikovsky had conducted his *Marche Solennelle* on the hall's opening night, where Stravinsky made his U.S. debut, where Benny Goodman swung with his integrated band, where Judy Garland crooned and Bill Haley kicked off the rock 'n' roll era. A press officer insisted that the Beatles regarded the place as "simply another theater, like the Albert Hall or the Finsbury Park Astoria," but that was so much blather. They knew the hall's importance and its import to their legacy.

How do you get to Carnegie Hall? The Beatles' story gave it an unconventional punch line. The gig was the brainchild of a music agent

Heading to the stage door of Carnegie Hall. Bill Haley & the Comets and Bo Diddley were the only rock 'n' roll acts that had been there before. If the Beatles were in awe of the place, they didn't show it.

named Sid Bernstein, who was convinced the Beatles could sell out the theater before he had ever heard them sing a note. Bernstein was a dynamo, a city-styled hustler who had grown up in New York City during the Depression and gravitated to Harlem's rich music scene as a journalism student at Columbia University. The streets were alive with the highball of jazz and blues—Bessie Smith, Billie Holiday, Fats Waller, Count Basie, Cab Calloway, Coleman Hawkins appeared in the warren of tiny clubs—and Bernstein became intoxicated. He took over a ballroom in Brooklyn that showcased Latin legends such as Tito Puente and Esy Morales, the latter of whom Bernstein eventually managed. Later he joined GAC (General Artists Corp.), booking its roster of Latin, jazz and R&B acts. On the strength of his successes with Judy Garland and Tony Bennett, he took over the agency's teen department, which included Bobby Darin, Bobby Rydell, Dion and Chubby Checker.

During the evenings, when his presence wasn't required backstage at a show, Bernstein haunted the New School's adult-enrichment courses, one of which was a lecture on Western civilization given by the famed syndicated columnist Max Lerner. Lerner insisted that each student read a British newspaper once a week to gain insight

into parliamentary-style government. "After a while," Bernstein recalled, "I started to see in the slim entertainment pages the name 'Beatles' popping up"—first in small print, later in the headlines. "And then the word 'Beatlemania' appeared."

That connected with the agent in him. His deep-rooted hustling instinct kicked into gear. If there was any substance to this Beatlemania business—any money to be made from it in America—Bernstein knew he had to get there first, before the competition beat him to the punch. That meant petitioning his bosses at GAC for permission to take on a new, untested act. But it didn't work. "They thought the name was crazy and gave me every excuse for not letting me go over [to England] to see them," he said. The agency's London representative assured them that "the group was strictly a local phenomenon."

If that was the way they wanted it, Bernstein thought, he'd make some inquiries on his own. He tried tracking down Brian Epstein, whose name had also appeared in the articles. "It took me three weeks of heavy detective work to get his phone number—Liverpool 6518," Bernstein recalled. When he finally got through, Epstein's mother, Queenie, put her son on the line.

It took next to nothing to tantalize Epstein. "I hit him with my experience," Bernstein explained. "Tony Bennett at Carnegie Hall, Judy Garland at Carnegie Hall." The names were like catnip to a man who idolized music-hall performers: "He knew about the tradition of Carnegie, about all the great artists who had appeared there." Epstein had just seen the movie *Carnegie Hall* on television and was in its thrall. Booking the Beatles there would be a link to tradition.

"Mr. Bernstein, how do you know they'll fill it?" he wondered.

Good question, considering that no one in America had heard of them. At the time, they were still without a record label in the States. Bernstein himself wasn't so sure. "Brian, a year from now they'll fill it," he said. "Let's make a deal." He offered $6,500 for two shows, and Epstein accepted. It was as simple as that.

They chose Feb. 12 for the performances, figuring that it was Lincoln's birthday, a school holiday, and the kids would be off. But it was still anyone's guess if American teenagers would be interested in the Beatles.

By January, Bernstein knew he'd struck gold. The Beatles had an American debut single that was zooming to the top of the charts and a commitment from Ed Sullivan. When Bernstein heard that, he said, "I knew I was home [free], because in those days, when you appeared twice on *Sullivan* you were a star." The Carnegie Hall shows sold out in a matter of hours. Tickets priced at $3, $4.50 and $5.50 were going for more than $100 on the street.

If the Beatles were in awe of entering the place, they didn't show it. Carnegie Hall was a beast of a building, a solid block of cocoa-colored masonry on the corner of Seventh Avenue and 57th Street that dwarfed everything around it. As far as legendary New York architectural structures went, it was up there with the Chrysler Building and the U.N. But the Beatles seemed quite calm about it. They relaxed in the prestigious green room just behind the stage, chain-smoking American cigarettes and drinking lukewarm tea, completely unfazed by the remarkable surroundings. On the walls just outside hung autographs of the hall's most famous denizens: Ravel, Rachmaninoff, Mahler, Caruso, Pons, Handy, Cliburn, Casals, Rostropovich, Callas … Quite a pantheon when you held them up against the four young Scousers lounging

WE'RE WITH THE BAND

There were so many extra requests for tickets that some privileged concertgoers (if not typical Beatles fans) got to sit on the stage. The boys were not happy with the arrangement.

backstage. Only a year ago, the Beatles were plying the woeful British cinema circuit. Now—this
august place. *How do you get to Carnegie Hall?*
They wouldn't dare take a crack at that one.

Until that night, Bill Haley & the Comets and
Bo Diddley had been the only rock 'n' roll acts to
set foot in Carnegie Hall. Apparently, its board
of directors didn't dig the groove. Neither Elvis
nor Buddy Holly was granted a date, not even
the Everly Brothers, whose sound was as tame
as 2% milk. Yet Bernstein seemed to have gotten
around the policy. "I knew the woman who did
the Carnegie bookings," he reminisced in 2008.
"I used to see her in the neighborhood supermar-
ket. I told her there was this group of four guys
from England who were a phenomenon. When
I made my application, she assumed they were a
string quartet—I never told her otherwise."

He might have advised her, "Roll over
Beethoven and tell Tchaikovsky the news." The
Beatles were about to rock Carnegie Hall off its
classical moorings.

A few minutes after 7, WMCA radio's "Good
Guys"—Joe O'Brien, Harry Harrison, Mitchell
Reed, Jack Spector and Dan Daniel—strode
onstage in an absurd attempt to introduce the
headliners. Each DJ had some pointless pat-
ter prepared: one-liners such as "Ringo saw
the Washington Monument, and he said, 'You
know, it doesn't look a thing like him.'" But it
was pointless in that acoustically ravaged hall.
As the lights went down, the 2,900 concertgoers,
most of them teenage girls, delivered a protracted
scream that never let up for the duration. "It was
mayhem," recalled Dan Daniel. "It was the most
piercing, uncomfortable sound I'd ever heard.
The five of us held our hands over our ears. Fifty
years later, my ears are still ringing."

The manic response had a similar effect on
the Beatles. You could see it in the way they com-
ported themselves onstage. Their timing seemed
herky-jerky; they were slightly off stride. There
was no way for them to connect through the
impenetrable wall of screams. Meanwhile, no
one in the seats could hear a word they sang. It

BERSERK AT CARNEGIE HALL

No one could hear a word they
sang through the wall of screams.
There was no way for the band
to connect. Eventually John
throttled the mike and yelled,
"Shut up!" It didn't do much good.

After the evening's second concert was over, the Beatles made a quick retreat from Carnegie Hall.

was absolute "bedlam" in that place, according to the editor of *Melody Maker*, who covered the show in an article aptly titled "The Night Carnegie Hall Went Berserk." A wild horde tore up and down the aisles, winging jelly beans mercilessly at George. Girls lobbed a jungle's worth of stuffed animals. It was a free-for-all, which the ushers watched with goggle-eyed horror.

The Beatles were used to such behavior. They'd seen it before—and worse, much worse—back home, but their music always managed to upstage the chaos. Not this night. If at first they were amused by the antics, they grew frustrated by the audience's refusal to listen. After the seventh song, John had had enough. The *New York Times* reported that he throttled the mike, "looked the audience sternly in the mouth, and yelled, 'Shut up!'" Not that it did him much good. "Yells and shouts rose to an ear-shattering volume," *Melody Maker* noted. After a concert lasting only 34 minutes—as with an identical show immediately following it—the Beatles bowed, dropped their instruments and headed for the wings.

THE PRESS DIDN'T HAVE MUCH to say about the performance per se. The "reviews" focused only on the event—the audience reaction, which was treated across the board as unruly teenagers run amok. Music wasn't on the agenda of the mostly middle-aged critics, who were not only mystified by the effects of Beatlemania but openly contemptuous of its appeal. The *New York Times* begrudgingly noted the band's "thumping, twanging rhythms" and referred somewhat evasively to "a ballad of tender intent." Nothing was said about the Beatles' talent. Only the *New Yorker*, at its condescending best, offered a backhanded compliment that defied logic. "They are worth listening to," its reporter conceded, "even if they aren't as good as the Everly Brothers, which they really aren't."

On the way out of the Headliner Club later that night, Ringo is waylaid by an amorous admirer.

For all the criticism, the Beatles couldn't have cared less. They'd written off the New York entertainment establishment as being largely ignorant of what they were about. It didn't really matter what was said about them in the press. The kids got the message. They connected with something visceral and personal, and that was nothing you could capture in print.

A savvy operator like Bernstein understood that. The next day, he called Epstein and suggested they go for broke. Bernstein proposed booking the Beatles into Madison Square Garden, where no musical act had ever performed. It was the granddaddy of New York venues, perhaps the most famous arena in America. One night, 22,000 seats; they could do it before the Beatles returned to London. All Brian had to do was to say the word and Sid would put his money where his mouth was.

"Do you think they could fill it?" Epstein wondered, dredging up the same timeless concern.

"You leave that to me," Bernstein said reassuringly.

He could hear the enthusiasm clicking on the other end of the line. It was so tempting, a huge payday for the Beatles. Maybe a springboard that would launch them onto some new Olympian plain. Epstein was genuinely struggling with a decision.

After an interlude he said, "Let's leave it for another time, Sid." It seemed like too much of a rush job to organize in a week, and frankly, Epstein doubted they could fill such a large arena.

Same old story, Bernstein thought. He'd heard it from naysayers who warned him against booking a has-been like Tony Bennett at Carnegie Hall in 1962, and again earlier that year with the Beatles. Eight months later, in October 1964, he'd hear the same arguments from Shea Stadium officials who discouraged him from making another harebrained booking. Fifty-five thousand tickets for the Beatles, they scoffed. You must be out of your mind!

Here Comes the Sun

EVERYBODY INTO THE POOL

In a shoot for *Life* magazine, the Beatles good-naturedly frolicked in some very chilly water during a sudden cold snap. Fortunately, the Florida sun soon broke through. (The original color transparency of this photo disappeared from the Life Picture Collection in 1964; the surviving black-and-white image was colorized by a digital artist.)

The voice of Yogi Berra might have delivered the play-by-play of the Beatles' arrival at Miami International Airport on Feb. 13, 1964.

"Do you think anyone will be in Miami to meet us?" Paul asked Carol Gallagher, an attendant on National Airlines Flight 11. As it turned out, he didn't need to wait for her answer. From the window of the gleaming DC-8 on approach, they could see the human crush on the ground—the largest airport crowd of the Beatles' 1964 tour, anywhere from 7,000 to 10,000 screaming teenage fans, according to various news reports. It looked like déjà vu all over again.

Local police were ready for the turnout—or so they thought. Twenty officers had been deployed for security, ostensibly to protect the Beatles from their fans. Rocky Pomerance, the police chief, had been scrupulous in his strategic planning, calling the NYPD for last-minute advice.

But the Miami cops were no match for the kids, who stampeded through the barricades, shattered windows, broke down doors, smashed car roofs. It was a melee, unlike the previous encounters, ringing up more than $2,000 in damage. It was all the police could do to stuff the Beatles into limos before whisking them, with sirens screaming, across Biscayne Bay to the Deauville Hotel on Collins Avenue.

The Deauville was one of the grand old Miami Beach meccas, a tropical sun-washed hideaway, with a water view nearly all the way to Cuba. Yawning palm trees lined the entrance. Girls in bikinis lounged by the pool. "This was just the most brilliant place I'd ever been to," Ringo said. The others merely dismissed it as "paradise."

IN 1964, MIAMI BEACH was riding the crest of a heyday, the sand-swept getaway of Northern sun worshippers hoping to sit out the winter freeze. The hotels along Collins Avenue were booming beachfront art-deco palaces—the Fontainebleau, the Eden Roc, the Raleigh, the Deauville—with the most vibrant nightclub scene east of the Nevada state line. Wander into any of the hotels on any night and you might encounter Frank Sinatra and Sammy Davis Jr. appearing on the same stage, or Dean Martin and Joey Bishop, or Steve and Eydie. Comics played the hotels' smaller "rooms." Gambling was wide open; every hotel had a bookie. It was a fantasy world unto itself.

The Beatles settled into the spirit of the place. At the Plaza they'd basically been shut-ins, but here there was plenty of opportunity to soak in the sights. "We were real tourists," Paul acknowledged. They immediately slipped into matching terry-cloth cabana outfits—or "cozzies," as Liverpudlians called bathing suits—and hit the beach, attempting to seek out kids their own age. "It was a big time for us," Paul recalled, "and there were all these lovely, gorgeous, tanned girls." He whipped out his Pentax and began snapping photos of the comely flock, as well as the phalanx

SPECIAL GUESTS
Arriving at the Deauville Hotel, one of the art-deco palaces lining Collins Avenue, the boys sparked a degree of interest that by now was familiar.

WITH THE BEATLES
GETTIN' THE BOOT

Photographer: Lynn Goldsmith

"The Beatles were coming to Miami to the Deauville Hotel to perform on *The Ed Sullivan Show*. I had turned 16 two days before. My stepfather was in the hotel business and arranged for me to be in the lobby for their arrival. Little did he know I thought the Beatles were too 'goody-goody.' I was a Rolling Stones fan. I didn't want to disappoint him, since he thought this would be momentous for me. Besides, I decided it might be worthwhile, as I'd never seen the lobby carpet. We had just moved to Miami, and in the tour of hotels I was mesmerized by the wild designs in the rugs. I wanted to photograph them all. When the Beatles came through the lobby door, I remember lots of light flashes, but all I could see was their feet. There, on the wondrous carpet background, a river of dark and white swirls, were the most amazing shoes I'd ever seen. I took one shot. John Lennon asked, 'Don't you want our faces?' I looked at him, smiled and shook my head no. He winked. I think he understood I got just what I wanted."

Now celebrated for her portraits of rockers, Goldsmith has published 13 photo books, directed music videos and written and performed a quirky "self-help comedy" LP, *Dancing for Mental Health*, via her alter ego, Will Powers. Turns out the teen who once sniffed at the Fab Four has always been game for change: "When I went to see the Beatles, all these girls were screaming and screaming. I thought they were idiots," recalls Goldsmith, 65. "But before long, I found myself just like them: standing on my chair, tears streaming down my cheeks, yelling, 'George! George!'"

89

of armed motorcycle cops who stood nearby, at the ready. "We'd never seen a policeman with a gun," Paul said.

The next morning, Feb. 14, the Beatles went to work. They had a full day planned, beginning with a *Life* magazine photo shoot in the hotel pool. For practical purposes, the Deauville couldn't seal off the area from its other guests. Thus, the place was a mob scene, impossible to navigate. An appearance by the Beatles, let alone the Beatles in swimming trunks, would touch off a riot. At the last minute the comedian Myron Cohen, who was on the same *Ed Sullivan* bill as the Beatles, phoned a friend who lived nearby and asked if some people could use her pool.

"Fine, Myron, if it's important to you, but who is it?" she asked.

After a moment he said, "These four guys from England with the hair. The Beagles, the Bagels ..."

A short time later, two convertibles pulled up to a nearby bungalow with the entire entourage spilling out of the seats. The Beatles were "pale, skinny guys," recalled Linda Pollak, whose well-connected parents owned the house. "Very polite, they waited to be told what to do."

Despite a sudden cold snap that blanketed the city, Brian Epstein ordered them right into the pool. Such duties were routine business for the Beatles, who were a well-oiled publicity machine. "I asked them to sing. They sang, each in his own way," remembered John Loengard,

AFTERNOON OFF
Given the opportunity of a cruise aboard a luxurious yacht, they spent a precious few hours chilling out, temporarily relieved of their public roles as Beatles.

Life's photo editor in charge of the shoot. "Then they started turning blue."

As a reward, they were whisked off for an afternoon's cruise aboard the *Southern Trail*, a 93-foot yacht with a full crew, owned by the sofa-bed magnate Bernard Castro. By midday the tropical sun had broken through, allowing them to take advantage of the vaunted climate. They went for a lazy group swim in the ocean. Later, Paul sat behind the yacht's piano and banged out a few lines of their next single, "Can't Buy Me Love," for Murray the K, who had come south with the boys, their unshakable court jester. They basically chilled out, adrift, for a few exquisite hours, munching snacks and sipping their favorite cocktail, Scotch and warm Coke. Not Beatles, not in this particular milieu, just four fresh-faced northern England lads, far from the madding crowd.

Even they knew that wouldn't last long. By the time they docked in the bay marina, it was necessary to resume playing keep-away with the fans. They were due at the hotel for a 6 p.m. rehearsal for the upcoming *Ed Sullivan Show*, but—how to get there without getting mobbed? Fortunately, they were in the hands of a resourceful cop, Sgt. Buddy Dresner, who had been assigned to head their security detail. Dresner was a crowd-control expert who specialized in Miami Beach conventions, as well as high-profile visitors like JFK and Elvis. A project like the Beatles was his cup of tea.

With the Deauville entrances under siege, Dresner rented a Hertz truck and delivered the boys to the loading dock behind the hotel. "And I got Cynthia [Lennon] a black Cleopatra wig and white sunglasses so she could get in and out," he recalled. In all the hubbub, however, he had forgotten it was Valentine's Day, with no time to get his wife, Dorothy, a gift. That was all the Beatles needed to hear. Incurable romantics, Paul and George called the desk at the Deauville before heading down to the rehearsal and ordered flowers sent to her, with Buddy's signature.

What goes around comes around.

In a room off the pool at the Deauville (with George still in his swimsuit), they prepare for their next *Ed Sullivan* appearance.

Hours of nitpicking sound checks left them hungry, and Dresner knew just what to do. He'd had a couple of days in which to observe their preferences. "They ate strange," Dresner said. "Paul and George would sit down and order dessert. I'd say, 'You can't do that. First comes the salad, then the main course, *then* the dessert.'" These boys needed some TLC, so Dresner asked them how they felt about a home-cooked meal. It turned out that was exactly what they wanted.

Dresner called Dorothy and gave her the news. "How many are there going to be?" she asked.

Buddy did the math; aside from the boys, there was their entourage—roadies, management, Cynthia, sundry others. "Oh, about 21," he replied.

Add to that Dresner's own family. His wife didn't bat an eye. By the time all the guests had made their way to the house, a feast was waiting: salad first, as Buddy had instructed, followed by roast beef, baked potatoes, green beans, peas—then dessert, strawberry shortcake.

It was more than satisfying after a week of eating hotel food. And family was important to each of the Beatles, even if it happened to be other people's families.

Saturday, Feb. 15, was devoted to work and play. A short press conference in the Deauville lobby left the Beatles feeling frustrated and irritable. What was it with these American journalists? Their questions were even lamer than the ones back home.

"Ringo, why do you wear all those rings on your fingers?" someone asked for openers.

"They'd look funny through my nose, wouldn't they?"

When another reporter asked Paul who was responsible for his hairstyle, he answered, "Napoleon and Julius Caesar," before turning away in disgust.

The press refused to treat the Beatles as anything but a novelty. Hardly a word was being written about their music, which was at the top of all the U.S. charts. "I Want to Hold Your Hand" held fast at No. 1, "She Loves You" at No. 2; *Meet the Beatles* was the undisputed album best seller. Other singles were climbing fast. No one took them seriously, gave them credit for reinventing rock 'n' roll. Sure, it was fun being internationally famous, but they were getting tired of this routine.

Despite that, or perhaps because of it, they threw themselves into a long afternoon rehearsal. The Sunday-evening *Ed Sullivan Show* would be their final live appearance in America, and they were determined that it have a lasting effect.

They would be fine; no one was worried. But the audience was another matter. On Sunday, Feb. 16, the trouble began early. Kids began queuing for the 8 p.m. show by midafternoon. Too many, judging by the length of the lines. Somehow, the Deauville's Napoleon Room was

oversold—the number of tickets issued for the show far exceeded the available seats. Security guards began turning kids away. To make matters worse, two renegade groups—one from the University of Miami, the other from Detroit—joined forces in a "Stamp Out the Beatles" campaign and were determined to bollix up the festivities. Beatles fans tried shouting them down, which necessitated police intervention to avoid a riot.

Upstairs, on the 12th floor, the band was oblivious to the commotion. They were ready to rock but needed to eat something first. Fish! They wanted fish. They put in a call to room service. There was nothing that an order of fish and chips wouldn't cure. But this was Miami Beach, and what they got instead was gefilte fish. "They didn't know what it was," said Buddy Dresner, "and they weren't crazy about it."

Dresner was sitting in a chair by the window, working his way through a grilled-cheese

sandwich. The boys had never seen one of those before, either. Unlike the gefilte fish, however, the melted cheesy thing in Buddy's hand sure smelled good. "Suddenly," he said, "that's what they wanted."

Trouble was, they were 15 minutes from airtime. The phone in the room started ringing off the hook. Sullivan's producers were getting itchy; the Beatles were wanted right away. But they weren't moving until they got their grilled-cheese sandwiches. "The four [of them] sat there until room service arrived," Dresner recalled. "Then they ate their sandwiches and rushed downstairs."

Unbeknownst to the Beatles, a throng of disappointed teenagers had gathered outside the ballroom, blocking the band's access to the stage. Security guards tried to wedge a passageway through the crowd, but it was slow going. Inside, the show was already in progress. Sullivan was

ALL DRESSED UP

Attention from a makeup artist on the day of the show. A mass of teenagers congregated outside the ballroom where the performance was to take place; the Beatles had to force their way through and nearly didn't reach the stage in time.

onstage, into his windup, when he realized that his star attraction was missing.

"And now, here are"—he eyed the confusion at the back of the room—"the Beatles, right after this."

A commercial would give them the extra time necessary to battle their way to the front. "Right at the end of the commercial, the Beatles finally broke through," John Moffat, the show's assistant director, remembered. "They came running up the aisle, they got hooked up, and I believe there was one microphone that didn't get hooked up. But you couldn't tell because all you could hear was the screaming."

"She Loves You" was practically drowned out by the noise. The girls in the seats had seen a week's worth of antics, and they knew the drill, jacking up the hysteria. It seemed like madness to segue from the rocker into a ballad, but John managed to deliver a poignant reading of "This Boy"—until the end, that is, when his voice cut loose, touching off a fresh outbreak of delirium. The follow-up, "All My Loving," was asking for it, a splash of oil on ungovernable flames.

The acts that followed provided a mild sedative—Allen & Rossi, a couple of borscht-belt

FUN IN THE SUN

The boys partook of Florida's pleasures: riding a speedboat, water-skiing, swimming. But they knew that though they wanted to conquer America, they didn't want to become Americanized. Their persona was English, and they intended to stay true to it.

comics; singer-dancer Mitzi Gaynor; the Nerveless Knocks, this week's acrobats; and Myron Cohen. When the Beatles came back to close out the show, they did so with a knockout punch. "I Saw Her Standing There," "From Me to You" and "I Want to Hold Your Hand" were an unbeatable one-two-three combination, and when Sullivan introduced Sonny Liston from the audience (he was fighting Cassius Clay for the heavyweight title the following week), the champ had to admire their style.

The Beatles felt good about their performance. They'd done what they came to do: show Americans who they were. They'd given them a taste of the juice. They'd showcased the hits and their raffish style. Beatlemania got a decent exhibition; the American girls certainly did their part. Sullivan had established the group across the country as an unqualified pop sensation. Oh, sure, the reviews were shortsighted. The *Miami News* issued a particularly harsh opinion: "Their music is passable, the lyrics border on the inane, and the voices are indistinguishable from the hundreds of other groups who subject the human ear to organized cacophony." Otherwise, the Beatles chalked it up as a huge success and were primed to kick out the jams.

They didn't come to Miami to check out the retirement community. They had nearly eight days in paradise and wanted to sample its pleasures: to go out, experience the city, hit the clubs, unwind. One of their first stops was a lounge at the Deauville, where the comedian Don Rickles was the current attraction.

The Beatles started cutting glances at each other. What the hell was this all about?

Celebrating after the show. With them was the comic Don Rickles (seated), whose abrasive stage act would make them uncomfortable.

"Where are you from?" Rickles asked Ringo. When Ringo replied, "Liverpool," to absolute silence, Rickles scrunched up his shar-pei face and said, "Oh, hear the applause!"

For a moment, the comedian got distracted. Rickles spotted Liston at an adjoining table and went into a bit about the upcoming bout. "Well, if you ask me, Jack, I think the black guy will win," he said.

"We were all a bit taken aback," George recalled. "We were trying to keep a low profile ... and then suddenly he'd come back to our table, and we'd be nervous sitting there, and he'd say, 'Look at that great personality!'"

"We were not amused," Paul said. "He was a bit of a shock."

John, in particular, was embarrassed, ducking out early with Cynthia. The rest of the Beatles stumbled out of that club feeling as if they'd been assaulted. A late-night visit to the hotel's main showroom, where the singer Carol Lawrence was appearing, proved calming to their jangled nerves.

Frankly, they'd had enough of the Deauville. Stashed in the back of a refrigerated butcher's truck, they decamped to a private estate on Star Island, an exclusive celebrity enclave in

South Beach, with a guardhouse that offered a semblance of privacy. The owner of the house had left the place well provisioned. The Beatles swam in the heated pool, water-skied and fished off the dock. Improbably, they reeled in a few grunts. "I don't think they'd ever fished before," Dresner recalled. "I had to teach them. I also had to bait their hooks and take the fish off because they didn't want to."

There were other shiny toys at their disposal, including a speedboat, which Ringo took for an inaugural spin. While bringing it ashore at the end of his outing, he came to the realization that boats had no brakes. "I proceeded to bring it into port head-on," subsequently crashing into a jetty, he recalled.

There were still the requisite obligations—an in-depth interview with the *Saturday Evening Post*; a couple of phoners to important disc jockeys, including one to placate *American Bandstand*'s Dick Clark, during which the Beatles gratefully acknowledged their reception in the States. And more. Someone had gotten the idea to pair them with Sonny Liston for a can't-miss photo op, combining the two biggest stories in the country. Nice idea, except that Liston flat-out refused. The Beatles? The champ wanted no part of it. That left the only alternative. During a radio interview, Paul had predicted that Clay would win the bout, prompting an invitation from boxing promoter Harold Conrad to meet the fighter during a workout in his Fifth Street Gym.

The Beatles weren't the least bit interested in fighters; they had limited, if any, knowledge of Clay. Why would they agree to such a stunt? According to George, "It was all part of being a Beatle, really, just getting lugged around and thrust into rooms full of pressmen taking pictures and asking questions." Which is how, on Feb. 18, a week before Clay would upset Liston to take the world heavyweight title, they found themselves trudging up the stairs to the challenger's gym, chaperoned by their security detail and the sports journalist Robert Lipsyte.

At the time, few realized what a powerful

WHO'S THE GREATEST?
They knew little about Cassius Clay (the future Muhammad Ali), and he knew less about them. But they were all consummate showmen, and they had no trouble making the most of a photo op.

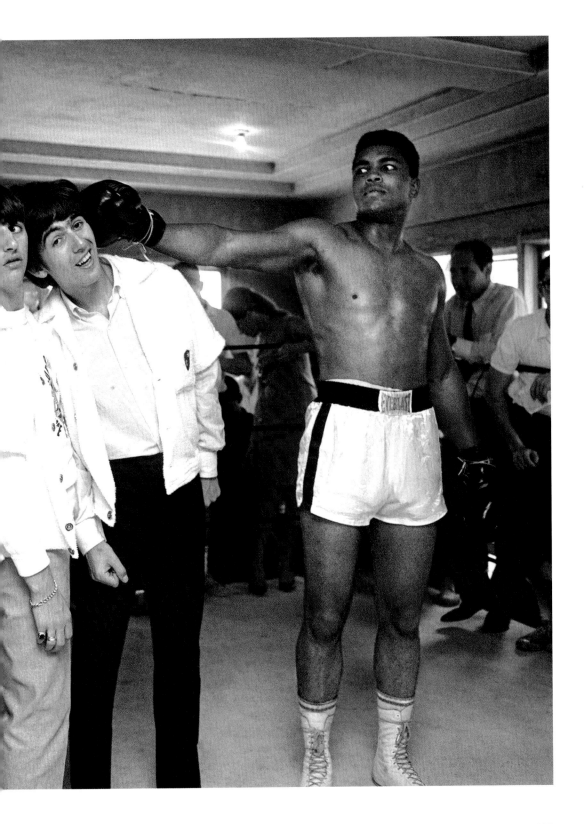

A young woman receives assistance at the Deauville after a sighting of the Beatles overwhelmed her.

figure Clay was—so powerful, in fact, that he would come in due time to be nicknamed "the Greatest," and, as Muhammad Ali, not only would be crowned *Sports Illustrated*'s sportsman of the 20th century but would emerge as an exemplar of racial and political freedom. All that most people knew then, however, was that he was an incorrigible motormouth, the Louisville Lip, who, as Norman Mailer claimed in *The Fight*, "could talk at the rate of three hundred new words a minute." Of course, the bulk of those words were silly strings of verse that Clay composed off the top of his head, as well as taunts that were alien to the boxing world. He referred to Sonny Liston as "the big ugly bear," claiming that Liston "even smelled" like a bear. "After I beat him," Clay bragged, "I'm going to donate him to the zoo." He was more entertainer than boxer, according to his detractors, who had no real grip on his potential in the ring. At least he had that much in common with the Beatles.

A boxing gym, however, was way out of their orbit. The place was foul-smelling and smoky, populated by characters who looked as though they'd stepped out of a Damon Runyon story. By contrast, the Beatles looked cartoonish, fey. For some reason, George, Ringo and John still wore the white terry-cloth waistcoats from their day on the water. "Get a load of them Beatles," grunted a ringside tough with a cigar clamped in the corner of his mouth. "They look like girls."

It didn't help matters that the boxer in question was nowhere to be seen. "Where the fuck's Clay?" Ringo asked, clearly annoyed. When told that he'd be back sometime soon, John bristled. "Let's get the fuck out of here," he said.

Nothing doing. There was too much of a publicity windfall at stake. To protect the opportunity, the security guards pushed the four Beatles and Lipsyte into a dressing room and locked them inside.

"They were cursing. They were angry. They were absolutely furious," Lipsyte recalled. They banged on the door, kicked at it, demanded to be let out. After a reasonable interval, when things calmed down, Lipsyte asked them how they thought Liston was going to fare. "Oh," John said, "he's going to kill that little wanker."

A few minutes later, when the door was flung open, the little wanker had morphed into one of the most gorgeous physical specimens anyone had ever seen. "Hello there, Beatles!" Cassius Clay roared. The guy had a smile as big as a car grille; he was teeming with charm. The Beatles were immediately captivated. The young boxer looked them up and down. "We ought to do some road show together. We'll get rich," he said.

He was a fireball, a spirit stamped for greatness and unspoiled by celebrity. The Beatles were putty in his hands, ready to be molded by Clay.

Good thing, too, because he had plans for the boys. First things first: into the ring. "Get down, you little worms!" he shouted at them, to which the boys dropped compliantly on their backs and wriggled. John was eager to fine-tune the act, instructing the boxer to straddle them "with his gloved hand in a victory pose." No problem for the ultimate showman. They all knew their roles and cues. Without any hesitation, Clay swooped down, scooped up Ringo, hoisted the skinny drummer over his head and swirled him in the air like a helicopter blade—*whoosh-whoosh-whoosh-whoosh-whoosh*. Clay's cornerman, Drew "Bundini" Brown, dropped to his knees and mock-pleaded for Ringo's life.

As tradition dictated, Clay stepped forward to deliver a few choice lines of verse:

When Sonny Liston picks up
the papers and sees
That the Beatles came to see me,
He will get angry and I'll knock him out in three.

It would never be published in the *Norton Anthology* or generate any classroom recitations, but the Beatles were delighted all the same. Clay's offbeat sense of humor, his ability to flip the bird at conformity while subverting the culture, made him something of a soulmate. "He had the whole crazy scene under his thumb," the Beatles told Brian Epstein after leaving the gym with great reluctance.

As Clay watched them depart, he cornered Lipsyte. "So tell me," he asked, "who were those little sissies?"

NEW YORK HAD BEEN AN EYE-OPENING experience, but Miami lay even further outside any world the Beatles had ever known. For a bunch of boys who hailed from a gritty, impoverished industrial port, having played gloomy Hamburg and rainy London, Miami was a whole other universe—sun and fun, slick borscht-belt showbiz, yachts, drive-ins, grilled-cheese sandwiches. This leg of their American journey introduced them to a culture radically foreign to their experience. Did it change them? Not essentially. They went back home and remained the Beatles, cranking out prototypical Beatles songs like "A Hard Day's Night" and "I Feel Fine." But meeting quintessentially American figures like Cassius Clay and Don Rickles, who understood how to project a consistent and unique persona, reinforced the boys' conviction that their own image, and staying true to it, was central to their fame. John, in fact, went ballistic when the photographer Dezo Hoffmann tried to get pictures of him water-skiing. The Beatles knew deep down that they were the Lads From London, and while they wanted to conquer America, they weren't about to become Americanized.

Determined to remain true to themselves, on Feb. 21 they boarded a Pan Am flight with a stopover in New York, and headed home.

Their hotel bills. Miami had exposed them to a world of wealth and pleasure that they'd never known.

CONQUERING HEROES:
THEIR RETURN AT HEATHROW

And in the End ...

THE BEATLES were elated when they got back to Heathrow early on the morning of Feb. 22. After a seemingly endless overnight flight in their rumpled suits—the same suits they had worn the day they left England—they stepped off Pan Am's "Jet Clipper Beatles" to an unprecedented welcome. If they had left London as explorers to the New World, they returned as conquering heroes.

They had anticipated a crowd similar to the one that had seen them off, but the 4,000 screaming, well-behaved fans they remembered had swelled to a mob of 8,000 to 12,000 whose pulse throbbed with nuclear pressure. Unaware of the sea change, the Beatles posed on the gangplank, mimicking the same choreographed wave they'd enacted two weeks earlier. The gesture pulled the pin on the crowd. It touched off a rampage through the airport that destroyed steel crash barriers, overturned bins and bashed in the roofs of cars without regard for propriety. Kids were trampled in the mad rush to reach the Beatles. Scores of girls fainted. A professionally painted banner— WELCOME HOME BOYS—lay shredded underfoot.

If the crowd had gone to a darker place, the Beatles hadn't. They saluted the assembled as "healthy and British and lads and mates and friends." Despite the violence, the homecoming was treated as a matter of national importance. The BBC interrupted its cherished afternoon TV sports show, *Grandstand*, to cover the Beatles' return, as did radio's *Saturday Club*, the tentpole of its Light Programme. Even the prime minister, Alec Douglas-Home, got into the act, naming the Beatles as his "secret weapon" in diplomatic relations with the Americans. No other British act had ever made such an impact in the States.

The trip to America had rocketed them to a new level of international fame. The question now was: Where would they go with it?

"I wasn't really aware of any changeover in our fame," George insisted. He claimed not to "think beyond the moment," to merely press on as before. But when we look back, it is clear that all the new sensations and insights the Beatles were exposed to—not only in America but inhabiting

*Everything in their world got careless and messy.
Months of bickering had dispirited them.
And despite that last, amazing concert on the
roof of their office building and the brilliant
Abbey Road LP, the Beatles disbanded.*

the epicenter of the '60s scene—contributed to their evolution as people and as artists.

Their first work when they returned to England was in the usual Lennon-McCartney mold. In fact, three days later they headed to Abbey Road studios to begin laying down tracks for "Can't Buy Me Love," "You Can't Do That," "And I Love Her" and "I Should Have Known Better." But soon enough they began to absorb influences that hadn't been part of their provincial Liverpool world. New, more introspective rock 'n' roll forms began taking shape in "I'm a Loser" and "Ticket to Ride," with reflective lyrics and irregular chord patterns that made more demands on their listeners. Songs emerged that sounded like nothing a rock 'n' roll band had

JAN. 30, 1969: ONE FOR THE ROAD

ever produced. Paul turned a lyric he called "Scrambled Eggs" into the signature ballad "Yester-day"; John contributed the gorgeous, poignant "In My Life" and his ambitious Dylan-inspired epic "Norwegian Wood," which Ringo described as a "mind-blower," owing to George's star-tlingly fresh infusion of sitar, the first ever recorded on a Beatles song. They had advanced the pop form with an inventiveness free of tired structures and gimmickry. For the first time, their producer George Martin explained, "we began to think of albums as art on their own, as complete entities."

Rubber Soul, Revolver, Sgt. Pepper's Lonely Hearts Club Band—they would change the course of popular music. They struck a groove that had never been reached before, in which the sound, the way a song was approached and recorded, played as important a part as the music itself. Their work began to reflect how each of them was experimenting with adulthood and '60s culture, incorporating their expanding interests—psychedelia, Transcendental Meditation, po-litical activism. But somehow the group pushed into new musical and topical frontiers while staying true to the core Beatles identity that had such mass appeal. Even though they were evolving, the world was changing with them and ready to welcome a more radicalized and musically sophisticated Beatles.

"Their body of work is amazing," Jann Wenner, the founder of *Rolling Stone*, told TIME.

They tapped into a revolution that was waiting to happen, releasing a pent-up primal scream, a burst of pure joy, not shaded by all the conflict that later came with it.

"They're like Gilbert and Sullivan were, with their cheekiness and subversiveness. They express all the feeling of the postwar baby boom in the English-speaking world, the freedom of expression which plays off all the excitement of growing up."

Later, the experimental changes began to take a toll as the Beatles started to grow up themselves, with individual points of view that didn't always coincide. John's drug use spun out of control. Paul's and John's sensibilities began to clash. George grew tired of the public maelstrom. Even Ringo's good humor couldn't make the center hold.

Their last work was fueled by personal resentment and clashes. Unable to resolve their differences in the studio through music, as they'd done earlier, Paul and John saw their collaboration morph into rivalry. They not only wrote songs separately but began recording alone, producing Beatles tracks for later mixing, as sessions for their albums grew more complicated, even hostile.

"I remember having three studios operating at the same time," George recalled. "Paul was doing some overdubs in one. John was in another, and I was recording some horns ... in a third."

Everything in the Beatles' world got careless and messy—not just their relationships but also their personal finances. By the end of the decade, John, Paul, George and Ringo knew the end was near. Months of bickering had dispirited them. John realized "there was no common goal anymore," and despite that last amazing concert on the roof of their office building and the brilliant *Abbey Road* LP, the Beatles disbanded.

Rock 'n' roll itself was on the wild end of the culture, but by the time the Beatles broke up the music had turned inward and a little scary. Within months Jimi Hendrix and Janis Joplin would be dead. Altamont had dealt a fatal blow to the '60s, and the ugly specter of Kent State lay on the horizon. The wider culture was in crisis as well; Bobby Kennedy had been assassinated, as had Martin Luther King, and the war in Vietnam had driven the world to extremes of disagreement. The Beatles had first come to the U.S. while the '60s were still naive and idealistic, like the Beatles' early songs. The decade closed with the group's acrimonious breakup and the revolution fully realized, though often marked by anger and division.

But in February 1964, it was a golden moment. The Beatles were innocents, and so was the time. We are left with that indelible impression—the moment when their bobblehead images materialized on the fuzzy TV screens across America and that drum lead into "She Loves You" kick-started an era.

It was a moment perfectly of its time, and yet it became universal. The Beatles tapped into a revolution that was waiting to happen, releasing a pent-up primal scream, a burst of pure joy, not shaded by all the conflict that later came with it. They set off that initial outburst and provided the soundtrack for all that followed—musical, cultural, social and political transformations.

Hard to believe that songs about holding hands and simple adolescent lust could set all that in motion. Their sudden appearance on the scene was sweet, it was unformed, it was exciting, it was a revelation. And dare we say it, it was *fun*.

It was Beatlemania—America never saw it coming.

Mirrorpix/Everett Collection

Credits

COVER
AP Images (Beatles at Plaza Hotel, Feb. 7, 1964)

BACK COVER
Ken Regan/Camera 5 (Beatles rehearse for *The Ed Sullivan Show*, Feb. 9, 1964)

ENDPAPERS
(Front) Arthur Schatz/Time & Life Pictures/Getty Images (screaming girls); (Back) Express Newspapers/Getty Images (Beatles with Sullivan)

TITLE PAGE
Mirrorpix (Beatles perform on *The Ed Sullivan Show*, Feb. 9, 1964)

CONTENTS
Mike Mitchell (Beatles press conference, Washington Coliseum, Feb. 11, 1964)

PROLOGUE
4 Photo collage by Sean McCabe; Larry Burrows/Time & Life Pictures/Getty Images (Vietnam helicopter); RB/Redferns/Getty Images (Chubby Checker); Keystone-France/Gamma-Keystone/Getty Images (Brandenburg Gate); United Artists (James Bond); Popperfoto/Getty Images (Soviet missile); Francis Miller/Time & Life Pictures/Getty Images (Martin Luther King); Michael Ochs Archives/Getty Images (Elvis Presley); David Farrell/Redferns/Getty Images (Beatles); 20th Century Fox/Getty Images (Elizabeth Taylor as Cleopatra); Keystone/Getty Images (JFK funeral); Bettmann Corbis (Gloria Steinem as Playboy bunny); John Cohen/Getty Images (Bob Dylan); Len Trievnor/Express/Getty Images (Muhammad Ali)

CHAPTER 1
8 © Harry Benson 10 Popperfoto/Getty Images 12 Harry Hammond/V&A Images/Getty Images 13 (top, clockwise from top left) David Redfern/Redferns/Getty Images; ABC Photo Archives/Getty Images; Michael Ochs Archives/Getty Images; Echoes/Redferns/Getty Images; Frank Driggs Collection/Getty Images; Michael Ochs Archives/Getty Images; (bottom, clockwise from top left) Terry O'Neill/Getty Images; Val Wilmer/Redferns/Getty Images; M. McKeown/Express/Getty Images; GAB Archive/Redferns/Getty Images; Val Wilmer/Redferns/Getty Images (2); Bob Thomas/Getty Images 14 (clockwise from top left) Evening Standard/Getty Images; Bettmann Corbis; Norman Parkinson/Sygma/Corbis; Bettmann Corbis 15 GAB Archive/Redferns/Getty Images 16 Courtesy of 45RPM Pictures Sleeves 17 Mirrorpix 18 Daily Mirror/Mirrorpix 21 (from left) Keystone/Getty Images; Mirrorpix

CHAPTER 2
22 AP Images 24 AP Images 26 Judd Mehlman/NY Daily News Archive/Getty Images 28 Courtesy of Adrienne Aurichio 29 Bill Eppridge 30 (from top) Dezo Hoffmann/© Apple Corps Ltd.; Michael

Ochs Archives/Getty Images 31 © Harry Benson 32 Bill Eppridge 33 Mirrorpix AP 34 (from top) NY Daily News Archive/Getty Images; Gilles Petard/Redferns/Getty Images 35 (from left) Rex USA/BEImages; Christie's Images/Corbis 36 Popperfoto/Getty Images 37 no credit

CHAPTER 3
38 Michael Ochs Archives/Getty Images 40 Bill Eppridge 41 CBS Photo Archive/Getty Images 43 Mirrorpix 45 (clockwise from top left) Ken Regan/Camera 5 (2); Mirrorpix; Ken Regan/Camera 5; AP Images; Daily Mirror/Mirrorpix; Bernard Gotfryd/Time & Life Pictures/Getty Images 46 CBS Photo Archive/Getty Images 48 CBS Photo Archive/Getty Images 50 Central Press/Getty Images 52 CBS 53 Courtesy of Billy Joel

CHAPTER 4
54 Henry Grossman 56 Cover from *Newsweek*, Feb. 24, 1964 © 1964 IBT Media. All rights reserved. Used by permission and protected by the copyright laws of the United States. The printing, copying, redistribution or retransmission of this content without express written permission is prohibited 57 Paul DeMaria/NY Daily News Archive/Getty Images 58 Michael Ochs Archives/Getty Images 59 Popperfoto/Getty Images 61 (clockwise from top) Popperfoto/Getty Images; Daily Mirror/Mirrorpix; TopFoto/The Image Works 62 (clockwise from top left) Central Press/Getty Images; Keystone/Getty Images; no credit 63 Bill Eppridge 64 Stan Wayman/Time Life Pictures/Getty Images 66 (from left) David Smith-Soto; Mike Mitchell 67–69 Mike Mitchell (3) 71 Daily Mail/Rex USA/BEImages

CHAPTER 5
72 NY Daily News Archive/Getty Images 74 Bill Meurer/NY Daily News Archive/Getty Images 76 (from top) AP Images; no credit 78 Popperfoto/Getty Images 81 Popperfoto/Getty Images 82 AP Images 83 Ken Korotkin/NY Daily News/Getty Images

CHAPTER 6
84 John Loengard/Time & Life Pictures/Getty Images, colorized by Sanna Dullaway 87 Bettmann Corbis 88 Courtesy of Lynn Goldsmith 89 © Lynn Goldsmith 90 Paul Gunther/MPTV 91 (from top) Daily Mirror/Mirrorpix; TopFoto/The Imageworks 93 Express Newspapers/Getty Images 94 Bettmann Corbis 95 Dezo Hoffmann/© Apple Corps Ltd. 96 Bob Gomel/Time & Life Pictures/Getty Images 97 Bob Gomel/Time & Life Pictures/Getty Images 98 Popperfoto/Getty Images 99 Dezo Hoffmann/© Apple Corps Ltd. 100 (clockwise from top) Dezo Hoffmann/© Apple Corps Ltd.; Bob Gomel/Time & Life Pictures/Getty Images; Dezo Hoffmann/© Apple Corps Ltd. 101 Dezo Hoffmann/© Apple Corps Ltd. 103 Express Newspapers via AP Images 104 Bob Gomel/Time & Life Pictures/Getty Images 105 Courtesy of Bruce Spizer from *The Beatles Are Coming!* by Bruce Spizer

EPILOGUE
106 Mirrorpix 108 © Apple Corps Ltd. 111 Stan Wayman/Time & Life Pictures/Getty Images

All photographs copyright as credited. No reproduction allowed without the express permission of the copyright holder.

TIME

Managing Editor Nancy Gibbs
Design Director D.W. Pine
Director of Photography Kira Pollack

The Beatles Invasion
Editor Roe D'Angelo
Designer Arthur Hochstein
Photo Editor Patricia Cadley
Reporter Mary Alice Shaughnessy
Copy Editor David Olivenbaum
Editorial Production David Sloan

Time Home Entertainment
Publisher Jim Childs
Vice President, Brand & Digital Strategy Steven Sandonato
Executive Director, Marketing Services Carol Pittard
Executive Director, Retail & Special Sales Tom Mifsud
Executive Publishing Director Joy Butts
Director, Bookazine Development & Marketing Laura Adam
Finance Director Glenn Buonocore
Associate Publishing Director Megan Pearlman
Associate General Counsel Helen Wan
Assistant Director, Special Sales Ilene Schreider
Brand Manager Bryan Christian
Associate Production Manager Kimberly Marshall
Associate Prepress Manager Alex Voznesenskiy

Editorial Director Stephen Koepp
Senior Editor Roe D'Angelo
Copy Chief Rina Bander
Design Manager Anne-Michelle Gallero
Editorial Operations Gina Scauzillo
Special Thanks Katherine Barnet, Jeremy Biloon, Susan Chodakiewicz, Rose Cirrincione, Jacqueline Fitzgerald, Christine Font, Diane Francis, Jenna Goldberg, Hillary Hirsch, David Kahn, Amy Mangus, Nina Mistry, Dave Rozzelle, Ricardo Santiago, Bruce Spizer, Adriana Tierno, Time Inc. Premedia, TIME Research Center, Vanessa Wu